5/10

World War II: Essential Histories

World War II

The Eastern Front 1941–1945

Robert O'Neill, Series Editor; and Geoffrey Jukes

ROSEN PUBLISHING®

New York

This edition published in 2010 by:

The Rosen Publishing Group, Inc.
29 East 21st Street
New York, NY 10010

Additional end matter copyright © 2010 by The Rosen Publishing Group, Inc.

Library of Congress Cataloging-in-Publication Data

Jukes, Geoffrey.
World War II: the Eastern Front 1941-1945 / Geoffrey Jukes.
    p. cm.—(World War II—essential histories)
"Robert O'Neill, series editor."
Originally published as v. 5 of The Second World War. Oxford: Osprey, 2002–2003.
Includes bibliographical references and index.
ISBN 978-1-4358-9134-0 (lib. bdg.)
1. World War, 1939–1945—Campaigns—Eastern Front—Juvenile literature. 2. Soviet Union—History—German occupation, 1941–1944—Juvenile literature. 3. Hitler, Adolf, 1889–1945—Juvenile literature. 4. Stalin, Joseph, 1879–1953—Juvenile literature. 5. Germany—Foreign relations—Soviet Union—Juvenile literature. 6. Soviet Union—Foreign relations—Germany—Juvenile literature. I. O'Neill, Robert John. II. Second World War. III. Title. IV. Title: World War Two.
D764.J85 2010
940.54'217—dc22

                                                                                    2009031235

Manufactured in Malaysia

CPSIA Compliance Information: Batch #TW10YA: For Further Information contact Rosen Publishing, New York, New York at 1-800-237-9932

On the cover: Soviet infantry crossing the Dvina River in Operation Bagration (*Imperial War Museum NYP 31136 PR2*)

Contents

Introduction 5

Chronology 7

Background to war
A dictators' deal and a double-cross 13

Warring sides
Germany gambles on a quick win 19

Outbreak
Germany achieves surprise 22

The fighting
Red Army battered but not beaten 23

Portrait of a soldier
The German and the Russian view 78

The world around war
Propaganda, Lend-Lease, and land grabs 81

Portrait of a civilian
"We were as mobilized as the soldiers" 84

How the war ended
Germany surrenders, Stalin joins the war on Japan 86

Conclusion and consequences
From alliance to Cold War 87

Glossary 91

For More Information 92

For Further Reading 93

Bibliography 93

Index 94

Introduction

After the Bolsheviks seized power in Russia in November 1917, Lenin expected revolutions to sweep Europe. Several occurred, but all were suppressed, and to retain power the Bolsheviks had to win a long and savage civil war, during which foreign powers intervened, Ukraine tried to gain independence, and Finland, Estonia, Latvia, Lithuania, and Georgia succeeded in doing so. Poland, previously partitioned between Germany, Austria-Hungary, and Russia, also became independent, in the process seizing territory in Belorussia and Ukraine. Russia's Far East provinces did not rejoin Russia until 1922, and Russian invasion ended Georgia's independence in that year. The Soviet Union, established on January 1, 1923, was internationally isolated as the world's only "socialist" state apart from its Outer Mongolian puppet. Most governments saw it as a pariah: conservatives because it constantly invited their subjects to revolt, socialists because its one-party dictatorship was alien to western Europe's and Scandinavia's democratic socialist traditions.

Russia therefore had to coexist with a hostile world, concluding peace treaties with its independent former provinces in 1920, and a trade agreement with Britain in 1921, then startling the world by signing in 1922 the Rapallo Treaty with Europe's other pariah, Germany. That treaty clandestinely helped Germany's rebirth as a military power. The Versailles Treaty of 1919 had limited its armed forces to 100,000, and banned conscription, military aircraft, tanks, and submarines. The Reichswehr's head, General von Seekt, saw cultivating relations with the nascent Red Army as a way to circumvent the restrictions.

The Rapallo Treaty gave Russia diplomatic recognition by Germany and the prospect of aid in restoring its ravaged economy, while Germany gained a food and raw materials supplier, and reduced dependence on its victorious enemies' goodwill. A secret agreement between the Reichswehr and the Red Army gave Germany facilities on Russian territory for testing, and training personnel to operate, weapons banned by Versailles, particularly tanks and aircraft. In return, Russia received substantial annual payments and access to information on designing, testing, and using weapons. Three secret centers were established: a flying school at Lipetsk, a tank school at Kazan, and a chemical warfare establishment near Volsk. To preserve secrecy, Germans attended only in small numbers, were temporarily recorded as having left the Reichswehr, traveled on false passports, did not wear uniform, and were forbidden after return to say where they had been or for what purpose. Russian officers were sent to Germany, where they undertook courses, attended maneuvers and war games, and were shown much of Germany's military industry, and they observed similar restrictions.

The schools were small. Lipetsk graduated only 120–130 pilots during its existence. But they worked intensively on tactics for interceptors, ground attack aircraft, and day bombers, and several of them became World War II "aces." The tank school accepted only 12 pupils per course, but they studied and tested the theories of armored mobile warfare advanced by Liddell Hart, Fuller, and Martel in Britain, and de Gaulle in France. German officers who went to Russia included future field marshals Brauchitsch, Keitel, Manstein, and Model, and several future generals, including the arch-proponent of mobile warfare, Heinz Guderian. The chemical warfare school conducted research into poison gases, anti-gas equipment, and antidotes.

Stalin abruptly ended this cooperation after Hitler came to power in 1933. Both armies by then had learnt much about each other, but the Germans benefited more, because in 1937–38 Stalin savagely purged the senior military. Most of those who had been to Germany were accused of spying for Stalin's exiled rival, Trotsky, or for Germany, Poland, and/or Japan, or plotting to lose a war and restore capitalism, and nearly all were shot. Their knowledge of the German army died with them, to be painfully relearned on World War II battlefields. Only in 1956, three years after Stalin's death, were the charges denounced as false; he had been protecting not the country but his own power, and that of his incompetent Defense Minister, Kliment Voroshilov.

Chronology

1941 **June 22** Germany invades; Italy and Romania declare war on Soviet Union.
June 24 Germans take Vilnius, the capital of Lithuania.
June 26–27 Finland and Hungary declare war on Soviet Union.
June 28 Minsk, the capital of Belorussia, taken.
July 1 Riga, capital of Latvia, taken.
July 8 Soviet West Front encircled southeast of Minsk; 290,000 captured.
July 16 Germans take Kishinev, capital of Moldavia.
August Stalin appointed Supreme Commander-in-Chief; Germans take 103,000 prisoners in Uman "pocket."
August 13 Siege of Odessa begins.
August 28 Tallinn, capital of Estonia, falls.
August 30 Germans cut all rail routes out of Leningrad.
September 8 Leningrad isolated except across Lake Ladoga.
September 10 Smolensk battle ends with Soviet retreat; Zhukov takes command at Leningrad.
September 16 Germans encircle Soviet Southwest Front, claim 665,000 prisoners.
September 17 Compulsory military training decreed for all Soviet males aged 16–50.
September 19 Germans take Kiev; siege of Leningrad (until January 27, 1944) begins; Germans launch Moscow offensive ("Typhoon").
October Germans encircle Bryansk Front; Stalin recalls Zhukov to Moscow and he arrives on the 7th.
October 7 Soviet West and Reserve Fronts encircled west of Vyazma.

October 8 Bryansk Front breaks out east, but 50,000 captured.
October 10 Zhukov appointed to command defense of Moscow.
October 13 Vyazma pocket liquidated; Germans claim 673,000 prisoners.
October 15 Decree on evacuating most of government from Moscow; rain, sleet, snow, and mud slow advance.
October 16 Last Odessa defenders evacuated by sea.
October 18 Germans enter Crimea.
October 19 "State of siege" (martial law) proclaimed in Moscow.
October 25 Germans take Kharkov; in Crimea, Soviets retreat to Sevastopol.
October 30 Siege of Sevastopol (until July 4, 1942) begins.
November 15 German Moscow offensive resumes.
November 17 Soviet counteroffensive in south begins.
November 20 Germans take Rostov-on-Don.
November 22 First supplies to Leningrad over ice of Lake Ladoga.
November 23 Germans reach a point less than 19 miles (31 km) from Moscow.
November 29 Soviets retake Rostov-on-Don.
December 5 Soviet Moscow offensive begins; continues until April 20.
December 19 Hitler dismisses 19 generals and appoints himself Army Commander-in-Chief.
December 25 Threat to encircle Moscow from the north eliminated; Kerch-Feodosia Soviet amphibious assault begins.

1942 January 2 Kerch-Feodosia assault ends; advanced about 60 miles (100 km).
January 7 Battle of Moscow ends after advances 60–150 miles (100–240 km).
January 8 Soviet general offensive begins; continues until April 20.
February 3 Germans encircle Soviet 33rd Army at Yukhnov.
February 6 German IX Army encircles 29th Army near Rzhev.
February 20 Two German corps encircled at Demyansk; supplied by air until relieved April 21–23.
March 19 Soviet 2nd Shock and 59th Armies encircled in Volkhov "pocket."
April 17 Soviet 33rd Army destroyed.
April 20 End of Soviet general offensive; Germans pushed back up to 200 miles (320 km) from Moscow.
May 3 Soviets begin attempt to re-encircle Germans at Demyansk.
May 12 Soviet Southwest Front attacks toward Kharkov.
May 16 Soviet Crimean Front, less 176,000 casualties, abandons all Crimea except Sevastopol.
May 23 German 1st Panzer Army closes trap behind Southwest Front.
May 29 Battle of Kharkov ends; Soviet losses 230,000.
June 28 Army Group South begins summer offensive.
June 29 Encircled 2nd Shock and 59th Armies destroyed; 33,000 captured.
July 8 Army Group South begins advance along River Don.
July 12 Stalingrad Front formed.
July 25 Battle for Caucasus begins.
July 28 Stalin's Order 227, "Not One Step Back."
August 10 Army Group A reaches Maikop oil field.
August 23 German VI Army reaches Volga north of Stalingrad.
August 26 Zhukov appointed Deputy Supreme Commander.
September 12 Germans reach center of Stalingrad.

September 20 Germans driven back across Caucasus mountain passes.
September 30 Germans advance along Caucasus west coast toward Tuapse.
October 9 Red Army Political Commissars replaced by "Deputy Commanders for Political Matters."
October 23 German advance on Tuapse halted.
November 6–12 Transcaucasus Front defeats last German attempt to reach Soviet oil fields.
November 11 Last German offensive in Stalingrad fails.
November 19 Southwest and Don Fronts launch Stalingrad counteroffensive's north pincer.
November 20 Stalingrad Front launches south pincer.
November 23 Pincers meet at Kalach, encircling 20 German and two Romanian divisions.
November 24 Kalinin Front begins offensive to prevent German transfers south.
December 12 German Stalingrad relief attempt begins.
December 16 Southwest and Voronezh Fronts attack on Middle Don; German Tuapse group defeated.
December 30 German Stalingrad relief force repulsed; Middle Don campaign ends; Italian VIII, Romanian III and Hungarian II Armies defeated; Army Groups Don and A threatened in rear.

1943 January 3 Army Group A begins withdrawal from Caucasus except Taman peninsula and Novorossiisk area.
January 8 Germans in Stalingrad reject surrender terms.
January 10 Reduction of Stalingrad "pocket" starts.
January 12 Attempt to lift siege of Leningrad begins.
January 18 Soviets clear south shore of Lake Ladoga and build railway along it to supply Leningrad.

January 24 Army Group A completes withdrawal from Caucasus.

January 30 South "pocket" at Stalingrad surrenders; Field Marshal Paulus captured.

February 2 All remaining forces in Stalingrad surrender.

February 16 Manstein launches Kharkov counteroffensive.

March 15 Manstein retakes Kharkov; Soviets retreat 60–90 miles (100–45 km), to Northern Donets river line.

April 8 Zhukov predicts German summer offensive against Kursk salient and recommends defense followed by counteroffensive.

April 12 Stalin accepts Zhukov's proposal.

April 15 Hitler issues directive for "Citadel" offensive against Kursk salient.

April 26 Soviets attack residual German forces in Caucasus.

July 5 Army Group Center begins "Citadel."

July 10 Allied landings in Sicily create threat to Germany in west.

July 12 Germans lose Prokhorovka tank battle – largest of war.

July 13 Hitler abandons "Citadel" and orders several divisions to west; Bryansk, Central, and West Fronts begin Operation Kutuzov, joined on the 17th by South and Southwest Fronts, on the 18th by Steppe, and on the 22nd by Volkhov and Leningrad Fronts.

July 27 Southwest Front held after taking bridgeheads over Northern Donets.

August 2 South Front offensive ended; small gains, heavy casualties.

August 3 Voronezh, Steppe, and Southwest Fronts attack south of salient.

August 7 Western and Kalinin Fronts attack on Smolensk sector.

August 13 Kalinin Front offensive temporarily halted.

August 18 Operation Kutuzov ends after advances of up to 95 miles (155 km).

August 22 Leningrad and Volkhov Fronts end offensive; few gains.

August 23 Kalinin Front resumes offensive; Voronezh and Steppe Fronts halt, after advancing up to 90 miles (145 km).

August 25 Battle for Dnepr begun by all five Fronts from Central southwards.

September 6 West Front halted after advancing 25 miles (40 km).

September 9 North Caucasus Front begins Novorossiisk–Taman offensive.

September 22 Voronezh Front seizes Bukrin bridgehead over Dnepr south of Kiev; South and Southwest Fronts halt after advancing up to 180 miles (300 km) and liberating industrial Donbass.

September 30 Central Front halts after seizing several bridgeheads over Dnepr.

October 2 Western and Kalinin Fronts end offensive after advancing 125–160 miles (200–260 km) and beginning reconquest of Belorussia.

October 9 End of Novorossiisk–Taman operation; Germans expelled from Caucasus.

October 10 Voronezh Front forces seize Lyutezh bridgehead over Dnepr north of Kiev; South Front begins clearing lower Dnepr's east bank of Germans.

October 14 South Front offensive successfully concluded.

October 30 Stalin signals readiness to join war against Japan after victory in Europe.

October 31 4th Ukrainian (ex-South) Front reaches northern approach to Crimea; Transcaucasus Front begins landing at Kerch, on eastern edge of Crimea.

November 3 1st Ukrainian (ex-Voronezh) Front attacks to take Kiev.

November 6 Kiev taken.

November 13 Army Group South pushes 1st Ukrainian back.

November 28 Tehran Conference of Allied leaders opens; ends on December 1.

December 19 Germans push 2nd Ukrainian Front back 12 miles (19 km).

December 22 1st Ukrainian Front stabilizes line after 25-mile (40 km) retreat.

December 24 Offensive by 2nd Belorussian and all four Ukrainian Fronts begins.

December Kalmyks deported for alleged collaboration.

1944 January 14 Start of offensive to end siege of Leningrad.

January 27 Siege of Leningrad ended.

January 28 About 70,000 Germans encircled at Korsun-Shevchenkovsky.

February 3 Leningrad Front forces enter Estonia.

February 17 Korsun-Shevchenkovsky battle ends; about 50,000 Germans killed, over 18,000 captured.

March 1 Leningrad offensive ends; Germans forced back over 130 miles (210 km).

March 28 2nd Ukrainian Front crosses River Prut into Romania.

March The Chechens and Ingush deported for alleged collaboration with the Germans.

April The Balkars deported for alleged collaboration with the Germans.

April 8 1st Ukrainian Front reaches Czechoslovak and Romanian borders; 4th Ukrainian Front and Independent Coastal Army attack in Crimea.

April 17 Offensive on Right Bank (of Dnepr), Ukraine, ends after advances of up to 300 miles (480 km) on a front of 920 miles (1,480 km).

May 9 4th Ukrainian Front takes Sevastopol.

June 10 Leningrad and Karelian Fronts start offensive against Finland.

June 23 Main Soviet "Bagration" offensive begins.

July 3 Minsk liberated, about 100,000 Germans encircled.

July 13 3rd Belorussian Front forces take Vilnius, capital of Lithuania.

July 28 1st Belorussian Front reaches Vistula and nears Warsaw.

August 1 1st Belorussian Front seizes bridgeheads over Vistula north and south of Warsaw; Polish Home Army launches Warsaw Rising.

August 7 4th Ukrainian Front enters Czechoslovakia.

August 23 2nd and 3rd Ukrainian Fronts encircle most of Army Group South Ukraine at Yassy-Kishinev.

August 24 Romania declares war on Germany.

August 28 3rd Baltic Front reaches German East Prussian border.

August 29 Official conclusion of "Bagration" and associated offensives; anti-German rising begins in Slovakia.

August 31 2nd Ukrainian Front enters Bucharest.

September 4 Finland breaks with Germany.

September 5 Cease-fire on Finnish front; Soviet Union declares war on Bulgaria; 2nd and 3rd Ukrainian Fronts reach Yugoslav and Bulgarian borders.

September 8 3rd Ukrainian Front enters Bulgaria; anti-German rising begins there.

September 9 Bulgaria declares war on Germany; 4th Ukrainian Front begins East Carpathians offensive.

September 14 Offensive by five fronts launched in Baltic area.

September 15 Soviet troops enter Sofia; Finland declares war on Germany.

September 20 4th Ukrainian Front enters Czechoslovakia, 2nd Ukrainian Hungary.

September 26 Leningrad Front forces capture Tallinn, occupy all mainland Estonia, reach Baltic coast, and isolate Army Group North.

September 28 3rd Ukrainian, Yugoslav, and Bulgarian forces begin Belgrade offensive; 2nd and 4th Ukrainian Fronts begin Budapest offensive.

October 7 Karelian Front begins drive to Norway.

October 10 1st Baltic Front reaches coast and cuts Army Group North off from East Prussia.

October 11 Hungary signs preliminary armistice.

October 16 German-backed coup in Hungary; army ordered to fight on.

October 20 3rd Ukrainian Front and Yugoslav forces take Belgrade.

October 22 Karelian Front enters Norway and liberates Kirkenes.

October 27 3rd Belorussian Front enters East Prussia.

October 29 Karelian Front halts and hands over to Norwegian Resistance.

November 2 2nd Ukrainian Front reaches southern approaches to Budapest.

November 9 3rd Ukrainian Front seizes bridgehead over Danube.

November 24 Baltic offensive ends; Army Group North isolated in Kurland.

December 3 3rd Ukrainian attacks north of Budapest.

December 26 2nd and 3rd Ukrainian Fronts encircle Budapest.

December 31 Soviets enter western suburbs of Budapest.

1945 **January 6** Churchill asks Stalin for offensive to ease pressure on Allies in Ardennes; Stalin brings Vistula–Oder operation forward by eight days.

January 12 1st Belorussian and 1st Ukrainian Fronts open Vistula–Oder offensive.

January 17 1st Belorussian Front takes Warsaw.

January 18 IV SS Panzer Corps attacks in Hungary, reaches Danube south of Budapest on the 20th, but repulsed on the 27th; 2nd Ukrainian takes Pest (Budapest east of Danube).

January 25 2nd Belorussian Front reaches Baltic coast (Frisches Haff), cutting Army Group Center's main supply or withdrawal routes; 1st Ukrainian Front seizes several bridgeheads across Oder.

January 28 1st Baltic Front and Navy take Memel (Klaypeda).

January 31 1st Belorussian Front seizes bridgeheads over Oder north and south of Kuestrin.

February 3 Vistula–Oder offensive ends; advance on Berlin to follow after removal of risk of flank attack from north.

February 13 Budapest taken.

February 15 1st Ukrainian Front crosses Neisse, encircling 40,000 Germans at Breslau.

February 16 German counterattack southeast of Stettin gains 5–8 miles (8–13 km).

February 18 Germans stop 4th Ukrainian's West Carpathian offensive.

February 19 Germans stop 2nd Belorussian Front in East Prussia.

February 23 1st Belorussian Front takes Poznan; Turkey declares war on Germany and Japan.

February 24 1st Ukrainian Front ends Lower Silesia campaign – heavy losses inflicted on IV Panzer and 17th Armies, Neisse river crossed on wide front; in Pomerania, 2nd Belorussian Front attacks; in Hungary, VI SS Panzer Army drives Soviets back over Hron River.

March 4 1st and 2nd Belorussian Front forces reach Baltic coast, cutting German Pomerania forces in two.

March 6 Army Group South attacks in Hungary.

March 16 2nd and 3rd Ukrainian Fronts counterattack in Hungary.

March 22 1st Belorussian Front widens bridgeheads over Oder.

March 26 3rd Belorussian Front wipes out encircled Germans at Frisches Haff.

March 30 3rd Ukrainian Front enters Austria.

April 2 3rd Ukrainian Front on southern approaches to Vienna.

April 5 Soviet Union informs Japan that 1941 Neutrality Pact will not be renewed.

April 6 3rd Belorussian Front begins storm of Koenisgsberg; fortress falls on the 9th.

April 13 Vienna taken.

April 16 1st and 2nd Belorussian and 1st Ukrainian Fronts open Berlin battle.

April 24 1st Belorussian and 1st Ukrainian Fronts meet in Berlin suburbs.

April 30 Hitler commits suicide.

May 2 Berlin garrison surrenders.

May 3 2nd Belorussian Front meets British, 1st Belorussian Americans, along Elbe; German forces in Bavaria and western Austria surrender to Americans.

May 5 Anti-German uprising in Prague; Stalin orders 1st, 2nd, and 4th Ukrainian Fronts to assist.

May 7 German High Command representatives sign unconditional surrender at Eisenhower's HQ in Reims; Stalin insists on a signing in Berlin.

May 8 Surrender ceremony in Berlin (Karlshorst).

May 9 Army Group North surrenders in Kurland.

May 11 Germans in Prague surrender.

June The Crimean Tatars forcibly deported for alleged collaboration with the Germans.

July 17 Potsdam Conference of Allied leaders begins.

July 26 Potsdam Declaration by USA, Britain, and China demands Japan surrender unconditionally; Stalin endorses demand.

July 30 Marshal Vasilevsky appointed Commander-in-Chief for campaign against Japan.

August 8 Soviet Union declares war on Japan and invades Manchuria, Korea, South Sakhalin, and Kurile Islands.

August 10 Japan accepts Potsdam Declaration and offers surrender provided Emperor retained.

August 14 Emperor proclaims surrender.

August 15 Anglo-American forces cease fire.

August 17 General Yamada, commanding Kwantung Army, asks Soviet terms.

August 19 Yamada unconditionally surrenders Kwantung Army.

A dictators' deal and a double-cross

In 1935 Hitler repudiated the Versailles Treaty and reintroduced conscription, and in 1936 he reoccupied the demilitarized Rhineland. Since his book *Mein Kampf* (My Struggle), written in 1924, advocated gaining *Lebensraum* (living space) for Germany in the east, Stalin saw a threat in German military resurgence, and sought British and French support for a "collective security" policy to restrain Germany. However, British and French reluctance to join one dictator against another militated against success. In April 1938 Hitler annexed Austria; in August he demanded that Czechoslovakia cede the Sudetenland, and threatened war if it refused. Stalin mobilized the equivalent of 90 divisions (far more than the 52 divisions

Germany then had), but the French and British governments coerced Czechoslovakia into surrender.

The Soviet Union was not invited to the Munich Conference that ratified the cession, so Stalin decided to seek a deal with Hitler. Secret negotiations produced on August 25, 1939, an agreement between the two Foreign Ministers, Molotov and Ribbentrop, which freed Germany's hands to invade Poland on September 1. A secret clause sanctioned Soviet annexation of territory that Poland had seized in 1920 east of the "Curzon Line," defined at Versailles as its appropriate eastern

Ribbentrop signing the Molotov–Ribbentrop Pact, watched by Stalin and Molotov. (AKG Berlin)

frontier, and on September 17, 1939, the Red Army invaded. Other secret clauses placed Finland, Estonia, Latvia, and Lithuania in the Soviet sphere. The three Baltic States were forced to accept Soviet military bases, and in 1940 were annexed.

Stalin did not intend to annex Finland, but in November 1939 demanded territory in the Karelian isthmus, to move the frontier back from Leningrad, and a base at Turku, on the entrance to the Gulf of Finland, offering in exchange about twice as much territory north of Lake Ladoga. When the Finns refused, he invaded and "recognized" a puppet Finnish "people's government" in Moscow. The Red Army prevailed in March 1940 by weight of numbers, but the Finns inflicted enormous casualties. The Red Army's inept performance encouraged Hitler's belief that Stalin's purges had "beheaded" it, and this belief became general also in British, French, and American military circles. The British and French governments contemplated sending an expeditionary force, ostensibly to aid Finland, but really to cut off Germany's supplies of Swedish iron ore. Only Finland's request for an armistice in March 1940 saved them from going to war with the Soviet Union as well as with Germany.

The Wehrmacht overran Denmark, Norway, Luxembourg, Belgium, the Netherlands and France in less than three months (April–June 1940), demolishing the rationale behind Stalin's deal with Hitler – his belief that German reluctance to fight a two-front war made the Soviet Union safe. At the end of July, Hitler ordered plans made for invading the Soviet Union in 1941. The invasion planning could not be entirely concealed. Bases and supply depots had to be established in East Prussia and German-occupied Poland, and Romania and Finland brought into alliance with Germany.

German activity did not go unnoticed by Moscow, nor were the Soviet espionage services idle. Two especially fruitful sources were a group of anti-Nazis in Berlin, members of the so-called Rote Kapelle (Red Orchestra), and Richard Sorge, a Soviet agent

in Tokyo, friendly with the German ambassador. Agents in frontier areas, and Soviet border guards, copiously reported German troop movements, and Churchill also sent warnings. However, several factors combined to give the Germans tactical surprise when they invaded on June 22, 1941.

Most important among them was a misinformation campaign. This included attempts to convince Stalin that German eastward troop movements were intended to distract British attention from renewed invasion preparations, and an offer to include the Soviet Union in the planned carve-up of the British Empire. This was made during Molotov's visit to Berlin in November 1940, and Stalin was sufficiently interested to ask Molotov twice whether there was any German follow-up. There was not.

Defense Minister Marshal Timoshenko and Chief of General Staff General Zhukov were uneasy enough to go to Stalin on May 15 and seek permission for a preemptive attack. Stalin asked, "Have you gone out of your minds?" and warned them that if the Germans were provoked into attacking, "heads will roll."

Some Russian authors blame this refusal for the early disasters. However, the circumstances cannot be ignored. The Soviet Union was internationally isolated following its recent acts of aggression. Only five days before Timoshenko and Zhukov went to Stalin, Hitler's deputy, Rudolf Hess, flew to Britain, and his flight could have no purpose other than to propose it make peace or even, given Churchill's well-known anti-Communism, join Germany's "crusade." Politically, the Soviet Union had to be seen as the victim, so preemption was impossible. Stalin believed invasion inevitable, but hoped to delay it by diplomatic maneuvers and punctilious observance of the economic agreements with Germany – Guderian later noted that as his troops lined up to invade on June 22, trainloads of Soviet raw materials were still crossing the border.

So Stalin's refusal to preempt was justifiable. Less so, however, were the lengths to which he went to avoid "provoking" the

Joseph Stalin, 1879–1953. General Secretary, Soviet Communist Party, from 1924, Prime Minister and Supreme Commander-in-Chief from 1941, Generalissimus from 1945. (AKG Berlin)

The rival invasion plans (a)

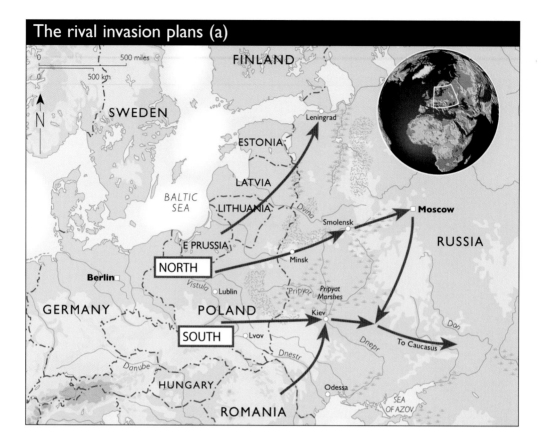

The rival invasion plans (b)

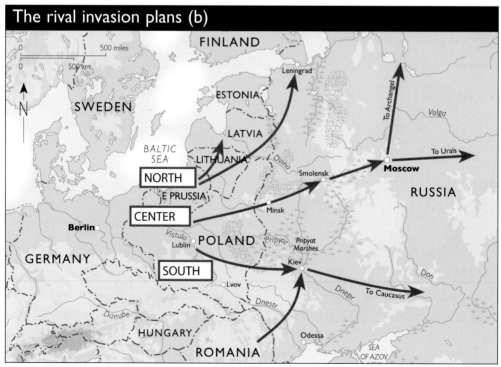

The rival invasion plans (c)

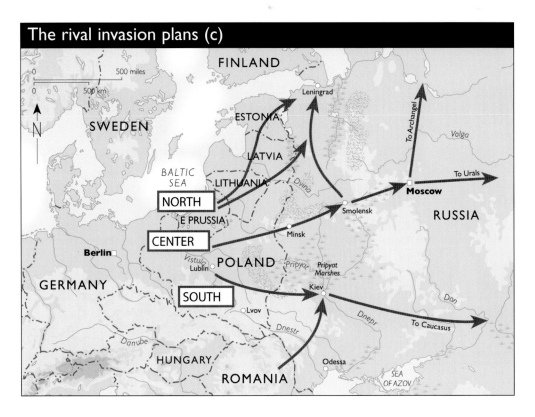

The rival invasion plans

(a) Produced by an Army High Command (OKH) team under General Marcks in early August 1940, aimed the main thrusts at Moscow and Kiev.

(b) Adopted by Colonel-General Halder, Chief of General Staff of OKH, on December 5, 1940. This added a strong thrust at Leningrad to Marcks' plan.

(c) Laid down by Hitler in Directive No. 21 (Operation Barbarossa) of December 18, 1940. This version of the plan made the destruction of Soviet forces in the Baltic States and the taking of Leningrad first priority. Moscow was to be considered only after this had been achieved.

Germans. When Kiev Military District's commander, Colonel-General Kirponos, occupied forward defensive positions, he was reprimanded and his orders annulled. The air defense forces were forbidden to attack German photographic reconnaissance aircraft that for weeks before the invasion regularly violated Soviet air space; even one that made a forced landing was immediately released. The fixed fortifications along the old Soviet–Polish border were dismantled before any new ones were completed. While the fate of the Belgian forts and Maginot Line in 1940 had shown the limits of fixed fortifications, their presence would at least have served to channel the invasion into fewer routes. Air force commanders were refused permission to disperse their aircraft.

There were also flaws in Soviet war preparations. Forces manpower more than trebled from 1.5 million in 1936 to 4.75 million in 1941, but officer-training schools' output only doubled. Training neglected defense, and was based on boastful slogans such as "beating the enemy on his own territory." The third was that faulty evaluation of Spanish Civil War experience prompted disbanding of the large tank and motorized infantry formations created in the early 1930s, and dispersal of their tanks as infantry support weapons. Following the achievements of the similar Panzer Divisions in 1939–40, Timoshenko began hastily reestablishing these formations, but few were ready by mid-1941.

All these deficiencies derived mostly from Voroshilov's incompetence as Defense Minister, though Stalin can be faulted for not dismissing

Commanders of the fronts during the concluding period of the war, 1941–1945: Left to right: I. S. Konev; F. I. Tolbukhin; A. M. Vasilevsky; R. Y. Malinovsky; G. K. Zukhov; L. N. Govorov; K. K. Rokossovsky; A.I. Yeremenko; K. A. Meretskov; I. Kh. Bagramyan. (Novosti [London])

him until 1940. However, two other flaws are directly attributable to Stalin. One was the purge of the senior military in 1937–38. This fell mainly on the younger generation of senior officers, and spared Stalin's civil war cronies, such as Voroshilov, Budenny, and Kulik. The coming war would show the latter to have learned little since 1920, while surviving members of this younger generation (such as Zhukov, Vasilevsky, Rokossovsky, Meretskov, Voronov, Malinovsky, Tolbukhin, and Rotmistrov) ultimately achieved successes outstripping Hitler's, or even Napoleon's, marshals. Those shot in 1937–38 probably included some equally talented, who, being higher up the "learning curve" in 1941, might have mitigated that year's disasters. But seeing how speedily the Germans in 1939–41 disposed of other armies that had not been "beheaded," it is unlikely that they could have avoided reverses altogether.

So the purge's effects should not be exaggerated. However, another of Stalin's errors was to veto the General Staff's defensive plan. This expected the main German thrust to come north of the Pripyat marshes, aiming at Leningrad and Moscow, with a secondary thrust south of them toward Kiev. Stalin insisted that Germany's primary objective was Ukraine's mineral and agricultural wealth, so its main thrust would come in the south. This can be explained only by Marxist economic determinism. In late summer 1941 Hitler indeed vacillated between Ukraine and Moscow. However, where the initial invasion was concerned, Stalin was wrong: Hitler deployed two army groups north of the Pripyat marshes, and only one south of them.

Germany gambles on a quick win

The German army began the Russian campaign following almost two years of outstanding success. Despite the prominence of Panzer (armored) and motorized infantry divisions, they constituted only a small part of the army, and achieved success by breaching enemy lines, then turning in to squeeze the enemy between themselves and infantry advancing on foot with horse-drawn artillery. Close tactical air support was provided by bombers, particularly the Ju87 "Stuka" dive-bomber, while fighter escorts ensured air superiority over the battlefield.

The plan was to destroy the Red Army west of the Dnepr River, in a four-month campaign starting in mid-May, concluded before the onset of winter. Events in the Balkans imposed a five-week postponement, but the invasion began at 3:30 am on June 22, 1941; if all went according to plan, it could still be concluded before winter set in.

The invasion force comprised three army groups, North, Center, and South, each commanded by a Generalfeldmarschall (field marshal). Its spearhead was four Panzergruppen (armored groups), two with Army Group Center, one with each of the others.

Army Group North (von Leeb) had 4th Panzergruppe, with three tank and three motorized infantry divisions and 20 of infantry. Center (von Bock) had II and III Panzergruppen, with nine tank and six motorized divisions, and 35 infantry divisions, while South (von Rundstedt) had I Panzergruppe, of five tank and three motorized divisions, 33 German and 14 Romanian infantry divisions. In Finland there were eight German and about 20 Finnish divisions. All formations were at or near full strength, but the Panzer divisions had only 200 tanks each, versus 400 in 1939–40.

The Army High Command (Oberkommando des Heeres, OKH) had a reserve of two tank, two motorized, and 24 infantry divisions. Including these, Germany committed 153 divisions (19 tank, 14 motorized, 120 infantry), Romania and Finland between them about 40 more. In manpower this meant about 3.3 million German and 500,000 satellite troops, with 3,300 tanks. Each army group had an attached Luftflotte (air fleet) of between 450 (North) and 900 (Center) combat aircraft, divided approximately 40–60 percent between fighters and bombers. With 55 German

Herman Hoth in 1941 commanded 3rd Panzer Group of Army Group Center. In 1942 he commanded the attempt to relieve Stalingrad. In November 1943 he was dismissed by Hitler for failing to prevent the Soviet recapture of Kiev. (Imperial War Museum)

Gerd von Rundstedt resigned command of Army Group South in December 1941, because of interference by Hitler, but was later appointed Commander-in-Chief West. (Imperial War Museum)

April 1940 Stalin replaced Voroshilov as People's Commissar (Minister) of Defense with Marshal Timoshenko, who tightened discipline, improved training, and began re-forming the large mobile formations that Voroshilov had disbanded in 1939. However, their reestablishment began only in March 1941, and less than half of the proposed 20 mechanized corps (each of one tank and two motorized infantry divisions) had been equipped by June. The Red Army had more manpower (about 4.75 million) and almost six times as many tanks as the Germans, but most were obsolete, or worn out; in June 1941 only about 40 percent were serviceable. The T-34 medium and KV heavy tanks, superior to the German Marks III and IV, went into production in 1940, but only

divisions and about 1,500 aircraft retained elsewhere, 73.6 percent of the German army and 58.3 percent of the Luftwaffe were committed to the invasion.

Germany's main deficiency was information. Despite almost daily reconnaissance flights beforehand, the invaders' maps were often inaccurate. Estimates of Red Army strength were good about the forces along the borders (assessed as 147 divisions and 33 brigades, versus an actual 170 divisions), but hopelessly wrong about capacity to mobilize and equip reserves. These errors would prove crucial after the quick victory failed to materialize.

The Red Army was being reorganized following the débâcle against Finland. In

In 1941 Ewald von Kleist's I Panzer Group advanced to Rostov-on-Don. By the end of 1942 he was commanding Army Group A in the Caucasus. Hitler promoted him to Field Marshal in 1943, but in March 1944 dismissed him. (Imperial War Museum)

Wilhelm Ritter von Leeb commanding Army Group North in 1941, encircled but could not take Leningrad and in January 1942 resigned over Hitler's interference with military decisions. (Imperial War Museum)

mid-1943 would the Soviet air force gain regular air superiority.

The navies played only supporting roles, and many Soviet sailors fought as infantry. The Soviet navy had more submarines than any other in 1941, but their performance was unimpressive. The surface forces' main function was to protect the army's coastal flanks, but the Baltic Fleet's loss of its forward bases in the first weeks forced its surface ships back to Leningrad. There they were boxed in by ice for half the year, and by a German mine barrier across the Gulf of Finland for the rest, though their guns contributed to shelling German positions. The Black Sea Fleet supplied and evacuated the garrisons of Odessa and Sevastopol, but did not prevent German crossings of the Kerch Straits from Crimea to Caucasus, or play any decisive role in the fighting along the Black Sea coast. The Northern Fleet helped escort Allied supply convoys, but British warships did most of that. The Pacific Fleet had little to do until 1945, and many of its sailors went west to fight as infantry. .

Alongside command-line officers the Red Army had a parallel "political officer" line. At different times they had veto powers over commanders, or were subordinate to them. They were responsible for political indoctrination of the troops and to some extent for welfare, but their basic function was to be the Party's watchdogs over the career military.

1,475 had been produced by mid-1941, and none went to border units.

The Luftwaffe had about 2,000 aircraft supporting the invasion, versus 12,000 Soviet, 8,000 of them in the European Soviet Union. However, most Soviet aircraft, too, were obsolete, serviceability was low, and 1,200 of those in the border area were destroyed on the first day, mostly on the ground. Not until

Germany achieves surprise

The definitive invasion order was Hitler's Directive No. 21, of December 18, 1940. It decreed Operation Barbarossa, "to crush Soviet Russia in a rapid campaign" (four months), and a "final objective … to erect a barrier against Asiatic Russia on the general line Volga–Archangel," from which the Luftwaffe could if necessary eliminate "Russia's last surviving industrial area in the Urals." All preparations were to be completed by May 15, 1941. Events in Greece and Yugoslavia delayed the start by five weeks, but a four-month campaign could still be over just before winter set in.

The Soviet leaders noted the growing German deployments along their western borders, but could not determine the invasion date. Not until Saturday, June 21, did they receive information definite enough to alert the border military districts. Timoshenko and Zhukov spent most of the evening and night writing orders; the local commanders received them only hours before the invasion, and many units remained unalerted. The air force suffered particularly, losing 1,200 aircraft on the first day. Navy Commander-in-Chief Admiral Kuznetsov ran through the streets from the General Staff to his headquarters, to put the entire navy on highest alert; in consequence, no ship or shore base was damaged in the first attacks, and no naval aircraft were lost.

Poor communications and transport hampered the army's attempts to react. Radios were few, so communications depended mainly on public telegraph and telephone nets, which were damaged or destroyed by bombing, gunfire, or German saboteurs. Many front-line units received no orders, others only orders already outdated by events. The mobilization plan required units to requisition trucks and horses from the civil economy, but the enterprises owning them took no steps to provide them.

Major-General (later Marshal) Rokossovsky, then commanding 9th Mechanized Corps in Kiev Special Military District (Southwest Front from the outbreak of war), learned that invasion was imminent only from a German army deserter. He had to open his secret operational orders on his own initiative, as he could not contact Moscow, District HQ in Kiev, or 5th Army HQ in Lutsk. His corps was mechanized only in name, with only one-third its allocation of tanks, those it had were obsolete, their engines worn out, and the "motorized infantry" had no trucks, nor even horses or carts. As his corps was retreating, it several times had to punch its way through German mobile forces. His only defense against the frequent air attacks was his own anti-aircraft guns, as he never saw a Soviet aircraft; and his corps' performance was so much above average that three weeks later he was promoted to command an army.

Red Army battered but not beaten

1941

The Germans achieved almost complete surprise. Army Group North (Field Marshal von Leeb), with XVI and XVIII Armies, totaling 20 divisions, and IV Panzergruppe (Colonel-General Hoepner) with three tank and three motorized infantry divisions, faced Soviet Northwest Front (Colonel-General F. I. Kuznetsov; "front" is Russian terminology for army group) with one army on the coast, and another inland. These had four tank, two motorized, and 19 infantry divisions, but the willingness of their soldiers, mostly from the former Baltic States' armies, to fight for their new masters was questionable.

Army Group Center (von Bock) confronted Soviet West Front (Army General D. G. Pavlov) in Belorussia. Bock had nine Panzer, six motorized, and 35 infantry divisions, while Pavlov's three armies had 12 tank, six motorized, two cavalry, and 24 infantry divisions. Bock planned for his two Panzergruppen (II and III) to advance 250 miles (400 km) into Belorussia and converge east of its capital, Minsk, to crush Pavlov's forces between themselves and the infantry of IV and IX Armies. Pavlov played into his hands by ordering all his reserves forward on June 24. By June 27, Pavlov's three armies, and a fourth sent to reinforce him, were encircled in two large pockets, around Bialystok and Novogrodek. Communications were so disrupted that Stalin first heard of the encirclement only three days later, from a German radio broadcast. He at once had Pavlov and several of his subordinates court-martialed and shot.

By July 8 the Germans had eliminated two Soviet armies and most of three others, taken over 290,000 prisoners, and captured or destroyed 2,500 tanks and 1,500 guns. Guderian took Smolensk from the south on July 15, while Hoth bypassed it on the north, closing the only eastward escape route on July 27. Some Soviet units broke out, but by August 8 347,000 prisoners had been taken, and 3,400 tanks and over 3,000 guns destroyed or captured. In the next two weeks another 78,000 prisoners were taken, and in two months Army Group Center had covered two-thirds of the 750 miles (1,200 km) from the frontier to Moscow.

The Germans now had to decide what to do next. Smolensk was not the victory Soviet historians subsequently claimed – it is now admitted that 486,171 (83.6 percent) of the 581,600 troops engaged there between July 10 and September 10 were "irrevocably" lost: that is, killed, captured, or wounded beyond further service. However, the Soviet resistance undoubtedly stiffened and German losses rose. With the additional stresses of distance, heat, and dust, over half of Army Group Center's tanks and trucks were out of action, and the infantry and the horses pulling their carts and guns were nearing exhaustion. The Barbarossa Directive had indicated that after "routing the enemy forces in Belorussia" the emphasis was to shift to destroying those in the Baltic, and taking Leningrad. Only after that would Moscow be considered. Hitler's adherence to this plan sat ill with Bock and Guderian, but he rejected their pleas to go immediately for Moscow.

Army Group South (Field Marshal von Rundstedt) had I Panzergruppe, VI and XVII Armies in Poland, and three armies (German XI, Romanian III and IV) in Romania. The five Panzer, three motorized, and 26 infantry divisions in Poland invaded Ukraine south of the Pripyat marshes, while the seven German and 14 Romanian divisions in Romania waited in case the Ploesti oil fields needed their protection, and did not move until June 29.

Stalin's belief that Ukraine would be Germany's main target had put more Soviet forces south than north of the marshes. Southwest Front (Colonel-General M. P. Kirponos) had four armies, and a newly formed South Front (Army General I. V. Tyulenev), along the Romanian border, had two. Between them they had 20 tank, 10 mechanized, six cavalry, and 45 infantry divisions, considerably more than the

Motorcycle troops were often used to lead the advance and test the reliability of their often misleading maps. (AKG Berlin)

invaders. However, their tanks, too, were mostly obsolete and worn out, the motorized infantry lacked trucks, and here too the Germans had air superiority, while the population in recently annexed Galicia, West Ukraine, Bukovina, and Bessarabia was mostly as anti-Soviet as in the Baltics and western Belorussia, facilitating free movement by sabotage groups. I Panzergruppe encountered Soviet tanks on the second day, and several battles delayed the required breakout, while the Soviet 5th Army, on being outflanked, retreated in good order into the marshes. Against South Front progress was also slow, and captures were few. The 400 miles (640 km) to the Dnepr took two months; Army Group Center had covered 500 miles (800 km) and taken many prisoners in that time.

However, Army Group South's fortunes improved after mid-July, when Rundstedt directed two of I Panzergruppe's three corps southeastward from Berdichev to Pervomaysk, to get behind three Soviet armies. XVII and XI Armies helped close this, the Uman "pocket," on August 2, and six days later 103,000 trapped Soviet troops surrendered. The rest of South Front had no choice but hasty withdrawal across the Dnepr, leaving Odessa as an isolated fortress.

In the first few weeks of winter the ice on Lake Ladoga would bear only sleighs. Not until the ice was 12 inches (300 mm) thick could trucks attempt the hazardous journey, as shown here. (AKG Berlin)

Argument about going for Moscow continued. Army Commander-in-Chief Field-Marshal Brauchitsch, Chief of OKH General Staff Colonel-General Halder, and Guderian all tried between August 18 and 24 to get Hitler's permission. Instead Guderian was sent south, to meet Kleist's I Panzergruppe at Lokhvitsa, about 140 miles (225 km) east of Kiev, and encircle the entire Southwest Front.

Three weeks earlier, on July 29, Zhukov had advocated pulling back Southwest Front and abandoning Kiev. Stalin refused, whereupon Zhukov resigned as Chief of General Staff and requested a field command. Stalin gave him the so-called Reserve Front, in the front line west of Moscow. Zhukov then forced the first German retreat of the war at Yelnya, but could not exploit his success because the fronts on either side of his had to withdraw. On August 18 he detected a sudden fall in German activity. Finding the same true of the adjacent Central Front, he told Stalin he believed Guderian was regrouping to drive south, and suggested establishing a strong force in the Bryansk area, to attack him in flank.

Stalin replied that he had foreseen the possibility by creating Bryansk Front a few days earlier. However, its commander, Colonel-General (later Marshal) Yeremenko, wrote in his memoirs that his directive was to defend against an eastward, not a southward, push. He failed to stop Guderian's tanks, and they met Kleist's on September 16. Two days later Stalin reluctantly authorized abandonment of Kiev, but too late; Kirponos was killed, his four armies were destroyed by September 26, and the Germans claimed 665,000 prisoners. Soviet historians rejected that figure, but post-Soviet official analysis admits "irrevocable" losses of 616,304 in Ukraine between July 7 and September 26,

Leningrad in the first winter of the siege. Corpses are being taken away from a collecting point. (AKG Berlin)

tantamount to losing over four divisions a week for 10 weeks.

While Guderian was returning north to prepare to advance on Moscow, Leningrad's defense was crumbling in Voroshilov's inept hands, and by September 8 it was completely isolated, except for a perilous route across Lake Ladoga. On September 9 Stalin sent Zhukov to take charge. By September 14 the Germans were on the Gulf of Finland, less than 4 miles (6.4 km) from the city's outskirts, so Zhukov had to act quickly. Three days of dismissals, blood-curdling threats, frantic improvisations, and probably some shootings rallied the demoralized defenders, and one piece of luck contributed – on September 12 IV Panzergruppe began leaving to join the Moscow offensive. On September 17 six German divisions tried to

break through from the south, but failed, and on September 25 Army Group North settled for a siege.

Stalin now needed Zhukov elsewhere. The assault on Moscow, Operation Typhoon, began on September 30, and immediately smashed through the defenders, Western, Bryansk, and Reserve Fronts. They numbered 1.25 million men in 96 divisions and 14 brigades, supported by two "fortified areas" (static defenses). But earlier losses had reduced their mobile forces to only one division and 13 brigades of tanks, with 770 tanks, and two divisions of motorized infantry. The rest included nine horsed cavalry divisions and 84 of infantry, with 9,150 guns, including mortars.

German losses so far had been comparatively small, 94,000 killed, 346,000 wounded, and very few captured up to August 26. But the Panzergruppen, now renamed Panzer armies, were seriously short of tanks. At the end of September, II had only 50 percent, I and III about 75 percent, of war establishment; only IV had its full complement. There was also a 30 percent shortage of trucks, and manpower in 54 of German's 142 Eastern Front divisions was over 3,000 (20 percent) below establishment.

Nevertheless, Army Group Center, reinforced by Panzer and motorized divisions from Army Groups North and South, and five infantry divisions from South, had 14 Panzer, eight motorized, and 48 infantry divisions, about half of all Germany's East Front force, outnumbering the defenders in tanks and aircraft (1,000 versus 360) by almost three to one, and in guns by two to one.

Guderian attacked on September 30, broke through Bryansk Front's southern flank, and advanced over 130 miles (210 km) in two days, to Orel. Bryansk Front's three armies were encircled by October 6, and on the 8th were ordered to break out eastward. Some did, but over 50,000 were captured.

Western and Reserve Fronts fared even worse. III and IV Panzer, IV and IX Armies attacked on October 2, and here too broke through at once, III Panzer (Hoth) heading for Vyazma, IV Panzer (Hoepner) for Yukhnov. On October 7 they met west of Vyazma, encircling 45 Soviet divisions, and by October 19 had claimed 673,000 prisoners. Post-Soviet research

ABOVE: The autumn rains turned roads to mud, making progress difficult. Here, German soldiers try to dig their vehicle out. (AKG Berlin)

BELOW: Progress was easier once the ground froze.

The front line at the start of Operation Typhoon

Front Line on September 1, 1941
Front Line on September 30, 1941
Direction of German advance

confirms a lower but still immense figure: 514,338 to the end of November, 41 percent of the two fronts' strength. On October 18 40th Panzer Corps took Mozhaisk, only 60 miles (100 km) from Moscow. Panic broke out in the capital on October 16; Stalin stayed, but government departments, the diplomatic corps, and most of the General Staff were evacuated to Kuybyshev (now Samara). Thousands of Muscovites fled, looting was widespread, and a "state of siege" (martial law) was proclaimed on October 19.

However, two factors intervened to slow the Germans. The first was the weather. Snowfalls began on October 6, and from the 9th sleet and heavy rain was almost continuous. Vehicles and carts bogged down, and the infantry, often up to their knees in mud, frequently outran their ammunition and rations. The weather was no better on the

Russian side, but the slowing favored the defenders, particularly by immobilizing the Panzers. The German advance could speed up again only after the mud froze, and low temperatures would then bring new problems.

The second factor was Zhukov, who arrived on October 7. Stalin at once sent him to the front line to establish the true state of affairs. At 2:30 am on October 8, he telephoned Stalin to tell him the main need was to strengthen the Mozhaisk defense line, then set off in heavy rain and fog to find Marshal Budenny and Reserve Front HQ. He finally found him in the deserted town of Maloyaroslavets, only to find that he did not even know where his own headquarters was, let alone the state of his forces.

On October 10 Hitler's press chief, Otto Dietrich, summoned the foreign press corps to announce officially that the war had been

Women digging anti-tank trenches at Moscow.
(AKG Berlin)

won. On that day Stalin gave Zhukov command of the remnants of Western and Reserve Fronts, and at his suggestion appointed Western Front's previous commander, Konev, as his deputy in charge of the front's northern sector, around Kalinin (now Tver). Stalin also acted instantly to reinforce the Mozhaisk defense line, transferring 14 infantry divisions, 16 tank brigades, and over 40 artillery regiments from reserve or other sectors, to re-form four armies. So eroded were they by previous fighting that they totaled only 90,000 men, equal to six full-strength divisions.

On October 17 the Kalinin sector, with three armies and one ad hoc combat group, became a separate Kalinin Front, under Konev. By October 18, the Germans had taken Kalinin and Kaluga, threatening to outflank Moscow from north and south, and

forcing Zhukov to re-form his front only 40 miles (64 km) from the city. Tens of thousands of civilians, mostly women and children, were conscripted to dig defensive lines, trenches, and tank traps; men were given a rifle and sketchy training, and formed into "people's militia" battalions.

November 7, the anniversary of the Bolshevik Revolution, was approaching. Stalin considered it important to hold the normal ceremonies, including a military parade in Red Square. To avoid disruption by air raids, the Party rally on November 6 was held underground, in the Mayakovskaya Metro station. Stalin's speech multiplied German losses by seven and divided Soviet losses by two, but most notably he invoked not Communism but Russian patriotism, then and at the parade on the next day. The troops marched straight to the front, with Stalin's exhortations to emulate "our great ancestors" – from Alexander Nevsky, victor over the Teutonic Order in 1240, to Kutuzov, who outwitted Napoleon in 1812 – ringing in their ears.

As the ground hardened in mid-November, the Germans recovered mobility, but met new problems. Few had winter clothing or white camouflage suits, and there were 133,000 cases of frostbite. Supplies of fuel, anti-freeze, and winter lubricants for aircraft and vehicles were inadequate. Frozen grease had to be scraped off every shell before it could be loaded, and maintenance of aircraft, tanks, and trucks in the open air was a nightmare. Stalin and Zhukov had ordered "scorched earth," as much destruction of buildings as possible, before retreats. The troops often went both frozen and unfed; at the end of November the offensive petered out.

The official German assessment of December 1, that the Red Army had no reserves left, now proved spectacularly wrong. From various sources, but particularly his spy Richard Sorge in Tokyo, Stalin had learned that Japan intended to attack southward, against Europe's and the USA's Asian dependencies, not northward against the Soviet Union. He began transferring divisions from the Soviet Far East; adding them to newly raised formations, he accumulated a 58-division reserve by the end of November.

Zhukov later admitted that he had not planned a major offensive. Local probing attacks simply revealed German weaknesses, justifying an offensive by West and Kalinin Fronts, and it began in 25 degrees of frost at 3:00 am on December 5. They had fewer tanks and aircraft than Army Group Center, but fresher troops, clad, fed, and equipped

for cold weather, guns, tanks, and trucks designed for it, and heated hangars for servicing their aircraft.

In 34 days of heavy fighting the Germans were pushed back a minimum of 60 miles (100 km), in some places up to 150 miles (240 km). Zhukov, supported by Chief of

Revolution Anniversary Parade, Red Square, November 7, 1941. The troops went directly from the parade to the front line, and so did the tanks. (AKG Berlin)

General Staff Shaposhnikov, set limited objectives, forbade frontal assaults, and wanted all resources concentrated on pushing the central front line back, to make Moscow safe for the next year's campaigning. But Stalin convinced himself that Germany could be beaten before the spring thaw, and on January 5, 1942, over Zhukov's and Shaposhnikov's objections, ordered a general offensive by five fronts. This began on January 8, continued till April 20 and achieved some successes, but at heavy cost

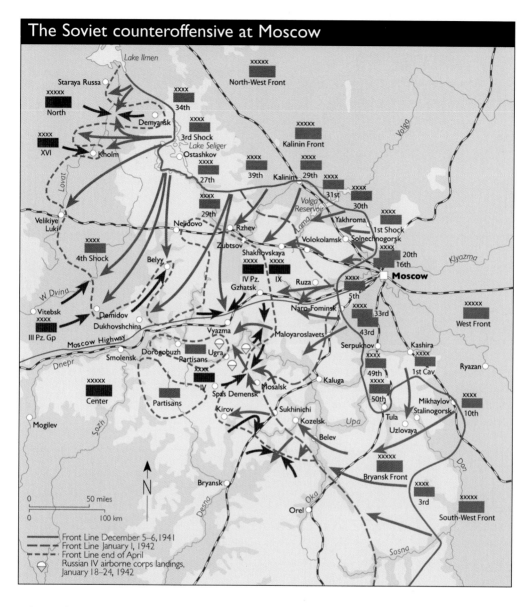

The Soviet counteroffensive at Moscow

Front Line December 5–6, 1941
Front Line January 1, 1942
Front Line end of April
Russian IV airborne corps landings,
January 18–24, 1942

compared to Zhukov's December offensive. Just over a million troops took part in each; 139,586 were "irrevocably" lost in December, almost twice as many – 272,520 – in the later offensive. Resources were so meager that some of Zhukov's artillery could fire only two shells a day. The average rate of advance was 1.5 miles (2.4 km) a day – minute compared

to what the Germans had achieved earlier and the Red Army would later.

Moscow was not Hitler's only problem. Army Group South was equally beset by weather, and was halted on October 11, 1941, as much by mud as by the seven armies of South and Southwest Fronts. On that day I Panzer Army reached the Mius River , but was halted by rainstorms and stiffening resistance. Further north, VI Army inflicted heavy losses on Southwest Front, forcing Stavka (Soviet GHQ) to permit withdrawal to the Donets River. This was a heavy blow to

the Soviet war effort because it meant abandoning much of the Donets basin, which then supplied about two-thirds of the Soviet Union's coal and iron, and three-fifths

ABOVE Moscow, December 1941. Abandoned German artillery. (Public domain)

BELOW The spring thaw rendered roads as impassable as autumn rains had done. (IWM)

of its steel and aluminum. However, much of the industrial equipment was removed to the Urals or Siberia, and the coal mines were dynamited; lost coal output was replaced by exploiting deposits elsewhere, particularly by forced labor in the north, at Vorkuta.

Rostov-on-Don, "gateway to the Caucasus," fell on November 20, but a Soviet counteroffensive had already begun, 56th Army attacking from the south, to keep the Germans engaged, while 37th Army attempted to strike south, to the coast behind them. Rundstedt ordered withdrawal to the Mius, about 50 miles (80 km) west, and this was already in progress when on November 30 Hitler countermanded it. Rundstedt thereupon resigned, and Hitler replaced him with Field Marshal von Reichenau, commander of VI Army and one of the few actively Nazi German generals. Both reluctantly accepted that Rostov could not be held, but Hitler ordered I Panzer Army to stand at an intermediate position east of the Mius. However, on December 1 the Soviets broke through, and Hitler had to permit retreat to the Mius. Rundstedt proved right. Army Group South held the line there easily until mid-1942, then advanced to Rostov and the Caucasus.

Hitler's reaction to the unforeseen Russian resurgence was to dismiss generals and forbid retreats. By December 19, Brauchitsch, Bock, Rundstedt, Guderian, Hoepner, and a number of others had gone, and he had taken command himself. Some German generals later conceded that his "stand fast" orders prevented the retreat from becoming a rout. But the front's stabilization owed at least as much to Stalin's overambitious offensive, and to the spring thaw; and Hitler's subsequent insistence on standing fast repeatedly condemned German forces to annihilation.

The Battle of Moscow was Germany's first major land defeat of the war, and marked the failure of Blitzkrieg. The Red Army had suffered enormous losses, but was still very much in business, and of 1941's three "symbolic" objectives, Leningrad, Moscow, and Kiev, only Kiev had fallen. Germany's

losses had been much smaller, but so was Germany's capacity to replace them. In the coming months, machinery evacuated to the Urals and Siberia would help the recently established industries there to begin replacing the equipment losses. From December, American entry into the war would provide the Soviet Union with a major supplier of the necessities of war.

1942

Kalinin and Western Fronts continued the "limited" offensive advocated by Shaposhnikov and Zhukov. But, ominously for Germany, a "limited" Soviet offensive even then meant a frontage of over 400 miles (640 km), and over one million men, in 95 divisions and 46 brigades. By April 20, when the spring thaw imposed a standstill, the Germans were well back from Moscow.

Hitler's plan for 1942 focused exclusively on the south. Almost all Soviet oil at that time came from three oil fields in the Caucasus, and reached the heartland by tankers up the Volga and railways along its banks. The Don, the European Soviet Union's second biggest river, sweeps through a right angle just south of Voronezh to run southeast for about 250 miles (400 km), before turning southwest to flow into the Sea of Azov. On this second "Big Bend" it is only 45 miles (72 km) from the Volga. The plan was for Army Group South to advance east along the Don, then cross to the Volga north of the major industrial city of Stalingrad, thus cutting the Soviet oil supply route. The second phase would be an advance into the Caucasus to capture the oil fields. This plan did not require Stalingrad to be taken, but Hitler wanted it because of its symbolic name (Stalintown).

Campaigning began badly for the Red Army. Marshal Timoshenko planned an offensive from a bulge in the line, the Barvenkovo salient, to retake Kharkov, then the largest German-occupied Soviet city, but did not know that the Germans were

The Soviet offensive at Barvenkovo took many prisoners, but the German counteroffensive took many more. (AKG Berlin)

planning Operation Fridericus, to eliminate the salient by driving across its neck from both sides. Timoshenko attacked on May 12, six days before "Fridericus" was due, and when only its southern pincer, I Panzer Army, was in position. Kleist hastily launched a "one-armed Fridericus" on May 17, and by the 22nd had closed the trap. Timoshenko sought reinforcements; Stalin said, "If they sold divisions in the market, I'd buy you some; but they don't," and again withheld permission to withdraw until too late. Three Soviet armies were wiped out, 29 divisions destroyed, many others badly mauled, more than 200,000 soldiers captured, and over 400 tanks lost, before the main German offensive even began.

An attempt to lift the siege of Leningrad also failed, with another army encircled and destroyed. Results were no better in the far south; efforts to prevent German access to the Kerch Straits, leading to the Caucasus, were a disaster with 30,547 lost, almost half of the 62,500 troops engaged.

For the main offensive, Bock had four German and four satellite armies. The northern pincer, along the Don, had

IV Panzer (Colonel-General Hoth) and
VI (Colonel-General Paulus) Armies. The
southern had I Panzer (Kleist) and
XVII (General Ruoff) Armies, and XI Army
(Colonel-General von Manstein) was to
become available after capturing Sevastopol.
Satellite armies, II Hungarian, VIII Italian,
and III Romanian, were to guard the German
flank along the Don. Bock had 89 divisions,
including nine Panzer, most at or near full
strength.

A brief panic erupted on June 19, when a
light aircraft, carrying a major with the plans
for the offensive's first phase, crash-landed
just behind Soviet lines. However, Stalin,

Soviet prisoner's-of-war digging along the roadside.
(AKG Berlin)

who in 1941 had wrongly believed Hitler would give economic targets priority, now declined to believe that Hitler was doing precisely that. On June 26 he dismissed the documents as misinformation, two days before the offensive began, precisely as they had outlined, with an attack on Voronezh.

Since that city could be the starting point for a northeastward push to Moscow, it was strenuously defended by 74 divisions, six tank corps, and 37 brigades, with 1.3 million men. Bock threw two of IV Panzer Army's three corps into an unnecessary attempt to take it, wasting their mobility until July 13. The Soviet defenders had over 370,000 "irrevocable" losses, but most of Southwest Front trudged off east along the Don, in relatively good order, with their heavy equipment intact. In pursuit was only VI Army, mostly on foot – its 18 divisions included only two Panzer and one motorized infantry divisions. For this Hitler dismissed Bock, and thereafter blamed him for all that followed, including the catastrophe at Stalingrad.

Hitler then divided Army Group South into Army Groups B (Weichs), to advance to the Volga, and A (List), to the Caucasus, and moved his headquarters from Rastenburg in East Prussia to Vinnitsa in Ukraine. From there he issued Directives No. 43 (July 11) and 45 (July 23), which envisaged seizing the Soviet Black Sea ports and Caucasus oil fields, thereby also cutting the Allied supply route through Iran. Directive No. 44 (July 21) ordered the Murmansk Railway cut. Had these objectives been attained, the only remaining supply route would have been across the Pacific and Siberia, and deliveries, except of aircraft, would have been approximately halved.

The pedestrian German pursuit produced few encirclements, and far fewer prisoners than expected. Hitler, however, ignored evidence that Southwest and South Fronts were withdrawing across the Don. On July 13 he ordered IV Panzer Army transferred to Army Group A, to cross the Don at Konstantinovka and move down its east bank to Rostov, to encircle Soviet forces he

believed still west of the river. Heavy summer rains and fuel shortages hampered movement, but anyway South Front had already crossed. In mid-July Halder confided to his diary that Hitler's underestimation of the enemy had become so grotesque as to make planning impossible.

The commander chosen for 62nd Army to defend Stalingrad city was Lieutenant-General V. I. Chuykov, till then Deputy Commander of 64th Army. During the

retreat he had observed German tactics'
heavy dependence on coordination – the
tanks not moving until the aircraft arrived,
the infantry not moving without the tanks –
and felt that the infantry's habit of opening
fire beyond the range of their weapons
suggested dislike of close combat. He decided
to try to keep his own front line so close to
the Germans that they could not use aircraft
and tanks for fear of hitting their own
infantry. That was easier said than done on

the steppe, but inside a large, mostly ruined,
city offered possibilities, provided Chuykov's
own men would accept the side effect of
increased exposure to small-arms fire. This
could not then be guaranteed, as morale was
low. It took threats, probably some
shootings, stirring messages from Front
Commander Yeremenko and his Chief

Fighting in the factory area at Stalingrad went on
throughout the battle. (Yakov Ryumkin)

Political Officer, Nikita Khrushchev, arrival of reinforcements, and Stalin's "Not one step back" Order 227 to produce results.

Once 62nd Army was inside the city, Chuykov made a second departure from orthodoxy. Fighting was mostly within buildings, often room-by-room, and the normal army structure of homogeneous platoons and companies was unsuitable. Chuykov reorganized 62nd Army into "storm groups" of 20–50 infantrymen, two or three guns, and one squad each of sappers and troops with flamethrowers or explosives. They studied enemy behavior, and where possible attacked when the Germans were eating, sleeping, or changing sentries. Assault groups of six to eight men, each carrying a submachine gun, 10–12 grenades, a dagger, and an entrenching tool (used more as a battle-axe than for digging), opened the attacks. When they signaled that they were inside, the reinforcement group followed, with heavier machine guns, mortars, anti-tank guns and rifles, crowbars, pickaxes, and explosives. It assisted the assault groups where needed, but its primary task was to cover the approaches against relief attempts. The third element, the reserve group, also had that function, but if not needed for that, it could split into assault groups and attack further. There was little scope for massed tanks or artillery, but single tanks or guns were used in support. Mining was first used against a building from which the Germans were firing on 62nd's only supply line, the ferries across the Volga. Sappers spent two weeks digging a tunnel to a point under the building, and three tons of explosives blew it and its garrison sky-high. Mining was employed extensively thereafter.

Not all the fighting was within buildings. The city stretched many miles along the Volga's west bank, and two large factory complexes, the Tractor and Barricades plants, were contested throughout the siege. A small hill, the Mamayev Kurgan, commanding the city center, was so intensively fought over that explosions made the ground too hot for snow to lie.

In such a narrow bridgehead there were no sanctuaries. Most of the Soviet artillery was deployed on the east bank of the Volga, directed by spotters in the city. There was no waterproof telephone cable, so communication with the east bank depended on ordinary cable that had to be replaced under fire every few days. Chuykov had to move his headquarters several times, finally settling in dugouts and half-submerged barges on the west bank, below some oil tanks that were found to be full only when a bomb set them on fire.

Attempts to repel the Germans by attacking northward were unsuccessful. On September 12 Zhukov returned from Stalingrad, reported this to Stalin, and then, while Stalin was studying the map, said to Vasilevsky, "We must find another solution." Stalin told them to find one and report the next evening. When they did, they put a proposal with two main points: first, they should keep the Germans forward by defending the city strongly, and second, they should assemble forces to encircle them by a pincer movement through the Romanian armies guarding their flanks, III north and IV south of the city.

The northern pincer would start from two bridgeheads on the southwest bank of the Don, at Serafimovich and Kletskaya. A tank force (5th Tank Army, under Lieutenant-General Romanenko) would assemble secretly in the Serafimovich bridgehead, to drive south toward the Don at Kalach, and the southern pincer would come north to meet it. Secrecy would be absolute – even Yeremenko, then commanding both Stalingrad and Southeast Fronts, was to be fed only generalities for the time being.

Preliminary reorganization saw Stalingrad Front renamed Don Front, and Lieutenant-General Rokossovsky appointed to command it. Yeremenko retained command of Southeast (renamed Stalingrad) Front, and a new Southwest Front was created in late October, deployed west of Don Front, and commanded by Lieutenant-General N. F. Vatutin. While 5th Tank Army would form the west side of the inner ring of encirclement, the rest of Southwest Front was to smash through the Romanians and

The Red Army springs the trap at Stalingrad

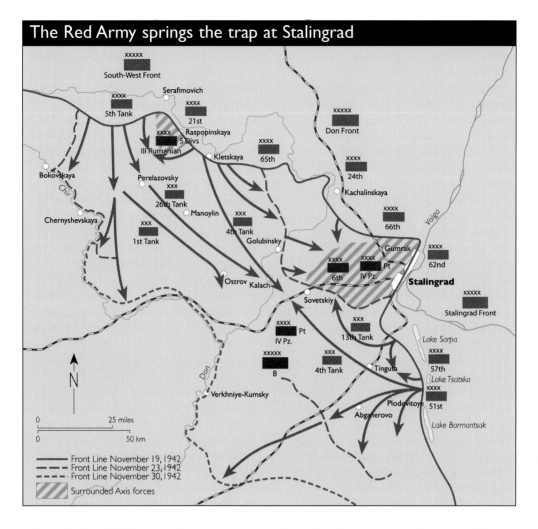

adjacent Italian VIII Army, to form a westward-facing outer ring against relief attempts. Zhukov and Vasilevsky estimated that assembling the required forces and supplies would need at least 45 days, so the counteroffensive could not begin until November. Stalin approved the plan, immediately sent Zhukov back to Stalingrad to scrutinize the northern sector, and a few days later sent Vasilevsky to the southern sector.

Exceptionally tight security was maintained, and no mention over telephone or radio was permitted. Zhukov, Vasilevsky, and other Stavka representatives shuttled between Stalingrad and Moscow, and reported orally to Stalin. The front commanders were informed in early October,

but subordinate commanders were told nothing until a month later. Whenever possible, troops, equipment, and supplies moved only by night, and the air force attempted to keep German air reconnaissance to a minimum.

The three fronts deployed 66 divisions and 19 brigades of infantry, eight divisions of horse cavalry, five corps and 15 brigades of tanks, and two mechanized corps, supported by six air armies. Not all units were at full strength, but the total, 1,143,500 men, 13,500 guns of 3-inch caliber or greater, and 894 tanks, was far more than OKH thought the Red Army could field. Such large movements could not be totally concealed, but the Germans realized neither their scale nor their purpose. The most that Colonel

Gehlen, head of the Intelligence Department "Foreign Armies East," achieved was a vague prediction of the northern pincer; of the southern he had no inkling.

An important part of the plan was an offensive by West and Kalinin Fronts, to prevent German mobile forces being transferred to Stalingrad. On November 17, Stalin sent Zhukov to command this; Vasilevsky stayed at Stalingrad to coordinate the three fronts.

In mid-September a renewed German offensive put 62nd Army into a desperate situation, relieved only through instant reinforcement by a division from Stavka reserve, and another six during October. The starting dates for the counteroffensive were set as November 9 for Southwest and Don Fronts, and November 10 for Stalingrad Front. However, late arrival of troops, ammunition, fuel, anti-freeze, horses, and other supplies caused a 10-day postponement.

Hitler dismissed Halder on September 24. His replacement, General Kurt Zeitzler, was more subservient, and even when, in the first week of November, evidence of a Soviet buildup opposite Romanian III Army began accumulating, OKH remained complacent. Hitler left for Berchtesgaden, to prepare his speech for the annual commemoration in Munich of his failed putsch of November 8, 1923. His headquarters began moving back from Vinnitsa to Rastenburg, and the cataclysmic events about to unfold could hardly have found German decision-makers worse placed to cope. On October 23 the British attacked in Egypt, and on November 2 Rommel's forces began retreating. On November 7 Anglo-American forces landed in French north Africa, so Hitler dispatched large forces to Tunisia, and on the 8th invaded Vichy France. On the 19th, the Soviet counteroffensive began.

Throughout this period Hitler was in the Berghof above Berchtesgaden, accompanied by only a few officers from his High Command, OKW, and none from OKH, responsible for the Eastern Front. The rest of his staff was divided between a barracks on the edge of town and his train in Salzburg

station. OKH was at Rastenburg; so was OKL (Air Force High Command), but its Commander-in-Chief, Goering, was in Paris. Hitler arrived back at Rastenburg late on November 23, and when Zeitzler met him with a list of urgent matters, Hitler attempted to put him off till the next day.

The Soviet decision to attack the satellite armies was deliberate. Germany lacked the reserves to man the long flank on the Don, and in the belief that the Soviets had no reserves, Hitler had entrusted its defense to (from west to east) Hungarian II, Italian VIII, and Romanian III Armies. The Romanians had fought well when recovering Romanian territory in Moldavia, Bessarabia, and Bukovina, but were less keen to die for Germany in the depths of Russia. Nor were they equipped to withstand the 80-minute bombardment by 3,500 guns that opened the counteroffensive at 6:30 am on November 19. OKH had "corseted" them with 14th and 22nd Panzer divisions. The latter had camouflaged its tanks as haystacks, and the hay attracted field mice, which carried off the insulation from the electrical wiring to line their nests. When Romanenko's T-34s attacked, many of 22nd Panzer's tanks could not be started. When they were, they, 14th Panzer, and the 1st Romanian Armored Division first attacked a secondary advance from the Kletskaya bridgehead. Only later did they take on 5th Tank Army, and to no effect. Five of Romanian III Army's 10 divisions surrendered on November 21.

The bridge at Kalach was taken by *ruse de guerre*. A column headed by several captured German vehicles drove up to it with headlights blazing. The bridge guards took it for the reliefs they were expecting, and were overcome almost before they realized their mistake.

The southern pincer, launched on November 20 by three armies of Stalingrad Front, also achieved total surprise and quickly smashed the German 29th Motorized Infantry Division and four of Romanian IV Army's seven divisions. Two mechanized corps headed toward Kalach, while one army advanced southwest toward the lower Don.

On November 23 the pincers met just south of Kalach, encircling German VI and part of IV Panzer and IV Romanian Armies, totaling 20 German and two Romanian divisions.

On November 22 Hitler ordered VI Army's commander, Colonel-General Paulus, to move his headquarters into Stalingrad and prepare to defend it. Paulus complied, but that day notified Army Group B's commander, Weichs, that he had very little ammunition and fuel, and only six days' rations. If supplied by air, he would try to hold out, but unless he could fill the gap left by the Romanians, he wanted permission to break out southwestwards. Weichs considered an immediate breakout imperative, and so did Paulus' five corps commanders. On November 23, Paulus, with Weichs' support, radioed Hitler, seeking permission to abandon Stalingrad. Hitler refused, bolstered by Goering's assertion on November 24 that the Luftwaffe could supply Stalingrad by air.

This was totally unrealistic. The minimum supply required to sustain the force was 750 tons (680 tonnes) a day, but the Luftwaffe's standard Junkers Ju 52 transport could carry at most 2.5 tons (2.26 tonnes), so at least 300 flights would be needed daily. Winter daylight was short, and of the seven Stalingrad-area airfields only Pitomnik could operate at night. Aircraft rapidly became unserviceable in the cold, and the transport fleet was heavily engaged ferrying reinforcements to Tunisia. These factors, and the certainty of Soviet attacks on the airlift, made Goering's promise nonsensical. On the day he made it, Wolfram von Richthofen, commanding Luftflotte 4, notified Weichs, OKH, and Goering of his dissent. Hitler chose to believe Goering, but Richthofen proved right: the best day's delivery was only 289 tons (262 tonnes), the average less than 100 (90.7 tonnes). The Soviets packed the airlift corridor with anti-aircraft guns and constant fighter patrols; between them they shot down 325 of the lumbering transports and 165 of the bombers used to supplement them.

On November 27 Hitler ordered XI Army from Vitebsk to the south, and its commander, Field Marshal von Manstein, to command a new Army Group Don. On paper it had four Panzer, 16 infantry, and two cavalry divisions outside encirclement, and 22 inside it. However, only one division (6th Panzer, transferred from France) was anywhere near full strength. Two other Panzer divisions had only about 30 tanks each, and the six Romanian divisions were little more than remnants. Nevertheless, Manstein planned a relief operation, letting Hitler believe he aimed to reinforce Stalingrad, but actually meaning to open a corridor for withdrawal.

The shortest relief route was from Verkhne-Kumskaya, about 40 miles (64 km). But it was the most obvious, the Russians could readily reinforce it, opposed crossings of the Chir and Don would be needed, and it would be vulnerable to flank attacks by 5th Tank Army. So Manstein chose a more southerly route, along the Kotelnikovo–Stalingrad railway. This was more than 80 miles (130 km) long, but had only small tributaries of the Don to cross. The route ran where the front ended in the Kalmyk Steppe, and only five Soviet infantry divisions were there.

Stavka, expecting Manstein to take the shortest route, sent 5th Shock Army to help 5th Tank disrupt the assumed preparations. Containing their probes across the Chir compelled Manstein to postpone the relief attempt from December 3 to 12. He planned for two Panzer divisions under Colonel-General Hoth to thrust northeastwards. Group Hollidt and Romanian III Army were to hold the Chir River line, 48th Panzer Corps to attack the forces facing Hoth from behind, and IV Romanian to protect Hoth's right flank. When Manstein judged the time right, Paulus was to attack to meet Hoth.

The Soviet command countered the plan at two levels. Locally, Yeremenko realized as early as November 28 that the relief attempt might come on his front, not where Stavka expected it. On that day his cavalry attacked 6th Panzer Division, detraining at Kotelnikovo, and established that it had come from France. Yeremenko at once contacted Stalin seeking urgent reinforcement, and began strengthening his southern flank. When Hoth attacked, on December 12, he advanced about a third of the way in two days, but on December 14 he encountered Yeremenko's tanks, and was stopped at the Myshkova River, about 30 miles (50 km) from Stalingrad. On December 19 Manstein ordered Paulus to break out toward Hoth, but Paulus refused, citing lack of fuel and Hitler's directive. Stavka sent two more armies into action on December 24, and in three days they pushed Hoth back beyond his starting point. Paulus' troops were now doomed.

Nor was that Manstein's only problem. Stavka's broader response to the relief attempt was a plan, approved on December 3, to slice through Italian VIII and Hungarian II Armies to the Black Sea coast west of Rostov-on-Don, and cut off Army Groups Don in Ukraine and A in the Caucasus. After Yeremenko's call for help, the plan was amended to highlight crossing Army Group Don's lines of communication and capturing the airlift's western terminals, Tatsinskaya and Morozovsk. On December 16 the offensive began, and within a week Italian VIII Army ceased to exist. On Christmas Eve Soviet mobile forces attacked the two airfields, and on December 28 Hitler sanctioned a general withdrawal to a line about 150 miles (240 km) west of Stalingrad. But the city was still to be held. At year's end he ordered SS Panzer Corps brought from France for another relief attempt.

1943

The troops in Stalingrad were starving and freezing to death. They had eaten most of their 7,000 horses, and their daily ration was down to 7 ounces (200 g) of horsemeat, 2.5 ounces (70 g) of bread, and half an ounce (14 g) of margarine or fat. On January 8 Voronov (Stavka representative) and Rokossovsky offered Paulus surrender terms, but he rejected them, so on January 10 Rokossovsky began Operation Koltso ("Ring")

to destroy the "pocket." Four days later Pitomnik airfield fell, leaving the airlift with only the secondary field at Gumrak. By nightfall on the 16th, the German-held area was sliced in two, and its area more than halved.

Gumrak fell on the 21st, and Paulus moved his headquarters from there to the basement of a department store in the city. On the 23rd Hitler again forbade surrender, and on the 30th promoted Paulus to Field Marshal, an implicit invitation to suicide, as no German Field Marshal had ever surrendered. On January 30 General Shumilov, commanding 64th Army, learned of Paulus' whereabouts and sent in tanks and motorized infantry, along with an Intelligence officer, Lieutenant Ilchenko. Shortly after they began shelling the store, a German officer emerged and told Ilchenko, "Our boss wants to talk to your boss." Ilchenko radioed Shumilov, who sent his Chiefs of Operations and Intelligence to negotiate. The southern "pocket" surrendered on January 31, the northern one on February 2. Nor was Stalingrad the only German setback. On January 13, Voronezh Front had smashed Hungarian II Army.

Axis losses in the Stalingrad campaign, including the fighting along the Don, included the whole of VI Army, part of IV Panzer, most of Romanian III and IV, and Hungarian II and Italian VIII Armies. In Stalingrad itself 91,000 surrendered, but weakened by starvation, cold, and typhus most of them died in captivity; fewer than 6,000 survived to go home. In the city, 147,200 German and 46,700 Soviet troops died. The Germans flew out about 84,000, mostly wounded, but many died in shot-down aircraft. The Germans' net loss (dead, captured, missing, or invalided, minus replacements) was 226,000, and the replacements were generally inferior to those lost. The surviving remnants of the Romanian, Hungarian, and Italian armies were withdrawn, an additional net loss of at least 200,000.

Soviet losses were not fully documented until 1993. In the defensive phase

A column of prisoners from Stalingrad plods off to prison camps. (AKG Berlin)

(July 17–November 18, 1942), 323,856 (59.2 percent) out of 547,000 engaged were lost. The offensive (November 19, 1942–February 2, 1943) took far fewer lives; of 1,143,500 engaged, only 154,885 (13.5 percent) were lost, and the fighting on the Don added another 55,874. Soviet losses therefore totaled 534,615, but they could be replaced from reserves and by conscripting males of military age in the recovered territories.

Army Group A had to leave the Caucasus except for the Taman peninsula and Tuapse–Novorossiisk coastal area. The original Soviet plan, to trap it by pushing down the Don to the coast behind it, had to be changed when the Stalingrad trap was found to hold over three times the numbers expected. More troops had to be retained there, and fewer sent down the Don. Army Group A thus escaped destruction; but its withdrawal ended the threat to the oil fields, and Nazi fantasies of advancing to the Middle East oil fields, and meeting in India the Japanese advancing from Burma.

A counteroffensive by Manstein, launched on February 15, achieved complete surprise, recovering much of the lost territory, including Kharkov, and forcing a Soviet withdrawal to the Northern Donets River. The spring thaw then imposed a lull.

The Soviet withdrawals created a huge salient, centered on the town of Kursk, and Hitler's plan for summer 1943 was to destroy the two Soviet fronts (Central and Voronezh) defending it. His desire for as many as possible of the new Tiger heavy and Panther medium tanks and Ferdinand self-propelled guns for the offensive, codenamed "Zitadelle" ("Citadel"), led him to postpone it several times, finally settling on July 5.

Soviet information on German intentions and deployments improved dramatically during that lull. No Soviet or post-Soviet source has ever explained why Intelligence improved so radically between mid-February and early April; but improve it did. By April 8 Zhukov was sufficiently confident that he knew the German plan to propose to Stalin strong defense of the salient to wear the Germans down, followed by a counteroffensive on the entire southern half of the front. After consulting front commanders Rokossovsky and Vatutin, Stalin accepted Zhukov's plan on April 12.

Hitler's plan received a mixed reception from the generals designated to implement it when they met in Munich on May 4. Model questioned the adequacy of the resources allotted; Kluge and Manstein wanted it launched soon, before Red Army strength built up even further. Guderian, now Mobile Forces' Inspector-General, totally opposed any offensive in the east. Axis forces in north Africa were only nine days away from surrender; an Anglo-American invasion of Europe was inevitable, and perhaps imminent. Guderian wanted to husband tanks for that, not squander them on the steppes. Hitler satisfied nobody. Model got only part of the extra resources he wanted. Kluge and Manstein did not get quick action, because Hitler waited until more new tanks arrived. Guderian would see most of the tanks he wanted destroyed at Prokhorovka on July 12.

The Soviet defenders received a windfall when a "Tiger" tank became bogged during trials on the Leningrad front. They captured it, and worked out how best to counter it. In the salient, troops and 300,000 civilians dug almost 6,000 miles (9,650 km) of trenches and anti-tank ditches, and thousands of foxholes. Six belts of defenses stretched back 110 miles (175 km) from the front line, with two more behind, manned by newly created Steppe Front, and a ninth along the east bank of the Don. Mines were laid at a density (2,400 anti-tank and 2,700 anti-personnel mines per mile [1.6 km] of front) four times that at Stalingrad, and there was more artillery than infantry in the salient, including 92 regiments from Stavka Reserve. To ensure adequate supplies a new railway was built, and over 1,800 miles (2,900 km) of roads and tracks were upgraded or repaired. Some divisions had been worn down in previous fighting to as low as 1,000 men, and reinforcements poured in.

A disabled Nazi tank in the area of the Prokhorovka bridgehead. (Novosti [London])

Central and Voronezh Fronts totaled 1,272,700 men, on a front of almost 350 miles (560 km), with 3,306 tanks and assault guns, 19,300 guns and mortars, and 920 of the multiple rocket launchers known to the Red Army as "Katyushas," and to the Germans as "Stalin Organs." In reserve behind them was Steppe Front, with 400,000 men and another tank army. These greatly outnumbered the 900,000 men, 2,700 tanks, and 10,000 guns of Army Groups Center and South. Hitler on July 2 ordered the offensive to begin on the 5th. That day Stavka warned both front commanders to expect the attack any time up to July 6.

German prisoners and deserters confirmed that the attack against Central Front was to begin at 3:00 am on July 5, after a 30-minute artillery bombardment. Zhukov was at Rokossovsky's headquarters, and when they learned this they began a counter-bombardment at 2:20. Zhukov would later conclude that this began too soon, before the German tanks and infantry occupied their starting positions. The assault began at 5:30 am, spearheaded by three Panzer divisions, with five infantry divisions in support. Model's troops advanced about 6 miles (10 km) that day on a 20-mile (32 km) front; but Rokossovsky had merely pulled back to the second defensive belt. The Germans gained little more ground, suffered heavy losses in men and tanks, and within two days were stopped.

Army Group South initially fared no better. Heavy rain during the night and most of next day made it hard to bridge streams and rivers, slowing both tanks and infantry. However, 48th Panzer and 2nd SS Panzer Corps penetrated the first line of Soviet defenses, and by nightfall on the second day had advanced about 7 miles (11 km). Vatutin, despite objections by Zhukov and Stalin, had dug his tanks into the ground to provide fire support for his infantry, so Stavka sent him the

The German plan for Operation Citadel

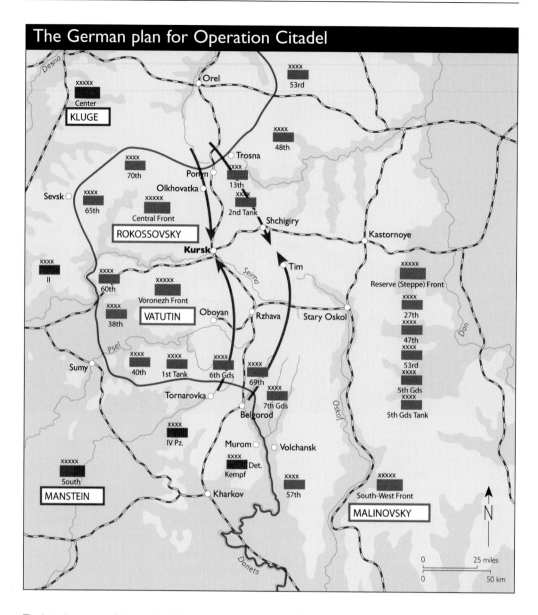

The intention was to eliminate the salient by the classic method, driving across its neck from north and south. However, the Soviets expected this.

5th Guards Tank and 5th Guards Armies from Steppe Front. On July 12 5th Guards Tank Army, with about 850 tanks and self-propelled guns, confronted 2nd SS Panzer Corps with about 600 near the village of Prokhorovka in the largest tank battle of the war. Losses on both sides were heavy, but the Germans withdrew, and thenceforth the Soviet tank generals had the whip hand.

On that day West and Bryansk Fronts, north of the salient, attacked toward Orel, threatening the rear of German IX Army, in Operation Kutuzov, the start of the counteroffensive. They deployed three armies initially, and when the Germans held those, committed another three.

Then events elsewhere distracted Hitler's attention. On July 10 Anglo-American forces invaded Sicily; clearly they would soon land on the Continent, and Italian enthusiasm for the war was evaporating. On July 13 Hitler told Kluge and Manstein he was calling

"Citadel" off and transferring a number of divisions to the west. Manstein objected, but in vain.

Mussolini was overthrown on July 25, and Hitler's suspicions that Italy would surrender or change sides were confirmed by radio intercept of a conversation between Churchill and Roosevelt. To shorten the line and free troops for the west, Hitler on August 1 ordered immediate evacuation of the Orel salient.

The second phase of the Soviet counteroffensive (Operation Rumyantsev) involved South and Southwest Fronts. To counter them Manstein sent much of his armor from the Kharkov area. No sooner had he done so than on August 3 Zhukov sent Voronezh and Steppe Fronts and the right wing of Southwest Front into the third phase, an advance toward Belgorod and Kharkov. The Germans were completely taken by surprise, and by August 5 had lost Belgorod and Orel. Reinforcements from Army Group Center, and the hasty return of some of the forces dispatched south, stopped the Soviet offensive temporarily. Hitler insisted on holding Kharkov and the Donets basin, but on August 7 the fourth phase of the counteroffensive (Operation Suvorov-1) began; West Front and the left wing of Kalinin Front launched 11 armies and several smaller formations towards Smolensk.

The vapidity of German belief that Soviet reserves were nearing exhaustion was evident. Figures released in 1993 showed that the eight fronts involved in the counteroffensive deployed 4,696,100 men, over four times as many as in the Stalingrad counterblow. Almost 358,000 of them were "irrevocably" lost, but this, at 7.7 percent of those engaged, was a significant improvement on the 13.5 percent of the Stalingrad offensive. The Wehrmacht's net manpower loss, 448,000, was almost double the 226,000 of Stalingrad.

The Kursk campaign was more decisive than Stalingrad in other ways also. It was the Red Army's first major summer offensive, and the Germans' last. After Stalingrad Manstein had mounted a successful large-

scale counteroffensive; after Kursk no German general could. From now on the Red Army had overwhelming superiority in men, tanks, guns, and aircraft, and would lunge from river to river, Dnepr to Vistula to Oder to Elbe, to meet the British and Americans. The enormous losses of 1941 had made the "Russian steamroller" a myth. Kursk restored it, and it became ever stronger, as territorial gains provided more recruits, while Germany's ability to replace losses declined, and its allies began melting away.

Steppe Front entered Kharkov on August 13, and after 10 days the Germans withdrew. The next Soviet target was the Donets basin. On August 27 Manstein attempted to make Hitler choose between reinforcing and abandoning it. Hitler equivocated. Italy was about to defect, so he had to find forces to occupy it and to replace Italian troops in the Balkans before the Allies gained a foothold. Of Germany's 277 divisions, 194 (70 percent) were on the Eastern Front, and the new commitments must be met mainly from them. Manstein had to withdraw behind the Dnepr, retaining bridgeheads east of it only at Dnepropetrovsk and from Zaporozhe to the coast.

The first Soviet "lunge" was to the Dnepr. Central, Voronezh, and Steppe Fronts, renamed 2nd Belorussian, 1st, and 2nd Ukrainian Fronts respectively in October, closed up to it on a front of about 375 miles (600 km) in the last 10 days of September. They seized bridgeheads on its west bank, then paused to regroup, resupply, and replace casualties. Between them they mustered 116 infantry divisions, 12 tank and five mechanized corps, and 12 brigades. Although still mostly a marching army, mobility, particularly speed of supply, was being greatly enhanced by American-supplied jeeps and 3-ton trucks, 434,000 of which were delivered in the course of the war. Their availability, and supplies of American machine tools, enabled the Soviet vehicle industry to build tanks at up to 2,000 a month, double Germany's best. To this array Army Group South could oppose

only 37 infantry and 17 Panzer or motorized infantry (now called Panzer Grenadier) divisions. All were severely below strength, and the Panzer/Panzer Grenadier divisions had only 257 tanks and 220 assault guns between them, an average of only 15 tanks and 13 assault guns per division.

On the Germans' heels, three Soviet armies in late September seized a bridgehead over the Dnepr at Bukrin, about 50 miles (80 km) southeast of Kiev, and in early October another army took one at Lyutezh, 20 miles (32 km) northeast of the city. The first attempt to recapture Kiev was made from the Bukrin bridgehead on October 16, but the Germans were expecting it, and in four days' fighting inflicted very heavy casualties, so Zhukov decided to make the next attempt from the northern bridgehead. This necessitated moving a tank army and

many artillery units up to 125 miles (200 km), crossing the Dnepr twice and the Desna once. So as not to alert the Germans, movement was mostly at night, and bad weather helped by grounding the Luftwaffe.

The offensive began on November 3, with two armies advancing from the bridgehead and their northern neighbor attacking in support. IV Panzer Army could not hold them, and Hitler dismissed its commander, Hoth. Kiev fell on November 6, and the Soviet advance continued, though with local setbacks, until November 26, when the autumn rains and mud temporarily immobilized both sides.

At the south end of the line, Vasilevsky coordinated offensives by 3rd and 4th Ukrainian Fronts, also to cross the Dnepr. The initial objective was the German east-bank bridgehead at Zaporozhe, held by

River, with substantial losses of tanks, and 5,000 prisoners.

But local German successes barely affected the big picture; Rokossovsky's Belorussian and Vatutin's 1st Ukrainian Front could potentially drive a wedge between Army Groups Center and South, then attack either in flank. To protect the junction with Army Group Center, Manstein on December 29 sent I Panzer Army north to join IV Panzer.

Since abandoning "Citadel," Army Group Center had been as hard-pressed as Army Group South. Kluge's troops were very thinly spread, and appeals for reinforcement from western Europe went unanswered, as Hitler wrongly believed an Anglo-American landing in France was imminent.

The terrain in the center and north of the front, peppered with forests, woods, and swamps, was far more suited to guerrilla warfare than the wide open spaces of Ukraine. Kluge therefore had to detach far more troops to guard his communications and fight partisans than did Manstein. During July and August the anti-partisan Operation Herman in Baranovichi province alone involved 50,000 Germans, most of them front-line troops.

Partisan warfare had begun in 1941, initially only as random attacks by bands of Red Army stragglers, but by mid-1943 it was large and organized enough to create considerable problems, particularly for Army Group Center. The partisans, depicted in Soviet-era accounts as heroes enjoying universal popular support, were often in reality an unwanted burden to the peasants among whom they operated. Villagers were equally liable to be killed by partisans for refusing support or by the Germans for providing it, and if partisans killed any Germans in the vicinity, the village was likely to be destroyed and its inhabitants massacred. As German reprisals increased, and the tide of war began turning against Germany, peasant support for the partisans increased, and by mid-1943 partisan operations were generally closely coordinated with those of the fronts. On August 3 the

Combined Soviet tank and infantry assault. (AKG Berlin)

part of I Panzer Army, and on October 10 three armies were hurled at it. By the 14th they had taken it, depriving the Germans of their only rail supply route to Army Group A in the Crimea. On October 23, 4th Ukrainian Front took Melitopol, and on the 25th, 3rd Ukrainian entered Dnepropetrovsk; by the end of the month both fronts were on the lower Dnepr, two armies were on the northern edge of the Crimea, and Army Group A was isolated. Simultaneously, 2nd and 3rd Ukrainian Fronts on October 16 began an offensive aimed at destroying I Panzer Army. They regained much territory, but a counterattack by 40th Panzer Corps (General of Mountain Troops Schoerner) retook Krivoy Rog, forcing 2nd Ukrainian Front back to the Ingulets

Partisan areas 1943–1944

FINLAND

Helsinki

Lake Ladoga

Gulf of Finland

Leningrad

Tallin

Lake Peipus

Lake Ilmen

Pskov

Riga

Daugava

RUSSIA

Rzhev

Moscow

Kaunas

Vitebsk

Smolensk

Tula

Minsk

Orel

Bryansk

Pripyat Marshes

Kursk

Don

Kiev

Berdichev

Kharkov

Dnestr

Dnepr

Zaporizhye

Dniepropetrovsk

Nikolayev

ROMANIA

Odessa

SEA OF AZOV

0   250 miles

0   500 km

BLACK SEA

N

Front Line July 1943
Areas controlled by partisan forces, summer 1943
Active partisan units outside partisan controlled areas

OPPOSITE: An example of the destruction that could be achieved by Soviet partisans. (AKG Berlin)

The open steppes of Ukraine offered little scope for large-scale partisan activity, and most groups there were small. In Belorussia and the Baltics, forests and swamps made it easier for partisans to form large bands and even to take control of sizable areas. They contributed notably to the Soviet successes at Kursk in 1943 and in Belorussia in 1944 by disrupting German communications and monitoring German troop movements. Some partisans in Ukraine and the Baltics were nationalist and fought Soviet as well as German rule. In February 1944 Ukrainian nationalist partisans ambushed and mortally wounded front commander General Vatutin. These anti-Soviet formations fought on until 1947.

"Rails War" began, in support of the offensive by West and Kalinin Fronts launched four days later. Its main targets were the railways supplying Army Groups North and Center; 167 partisan units with about 100,000 men took part, and it lasted until September 15, wreaking havoc with German supplies.

The front from the Karelian isthmus to the Arctic coast was held by the Finns and, at its northern extremity, German XX Mountain Army. The only democracy to join the Axis, Finland took pains to present its war as one not of conquest but of restitution, of territory lost in 1940; Finnish forces stopped at the 1939 frontier or first defensible position beyond it. They made no serious effort to cut the Murmansk railway, along which about one-quarter of all Allied aid passed, and to Hitler's fury, declined to join German efforts against Leningrad. Stavka maintained relatively small forces on the Finnish front, and waited for Finland to admit it had backed the wrong horse. Soviet peace proposals made in July 1943 were rejected, but Anglo-American pressure and the perception that Germany was losing combined to intensify Finnish efforts to leave the war. XX Mountain Army was potentially both an embarrassment and a hostage. On September 28 Hitler ordered it to hold northern Finland, especially Petsamo port and nickel mine, if Finland sought an armistice.

The "Battle for the Dnepr" ended on December 22. In a month's fighting, Army Group South pushed 1st Ukrainian Front back about 25 miles (40 km) from the line it had reached by mid-November, but could not stabilize a line along the Dnepr. On December 24, Stavka began the reconquest of right-bank Ukraine, using all four Ukrainian Fronts and 2nd Belorussian Front. With 188 divisions, 19 corps, 13 brigades, and 2,406,100 men, the five fronts had not much less than the Wehrmacht's total Eastern Front strength (195 divisions, 2,850,000 men). In tanks and guns they outnumbered the Germans by over three to one, and their growing superiority was marked by the breadth of their assault, on a front of over 800 miles (1,300 km).

1944

The Soviet advance in the south continued for 116 days. When it ended, on April 17, 1944, the front line had moved up to 300 miles (480 km) west since December. Despite the transfer of 34 German divisions from western Europe, the Red Army had reached the Eastern Carpathians, and taken the war into enemy territory by crossing into Romania.

Stalin had long come to accept Zhukov's and Vasilevsky's view that limited operations with clearly defined objectives were preferable to general offensives, by enabling resources to be concentrated. But it was now becoming possible not only to make "limited" operations very large, but also to mount two simultaneously. On January 14, with the advance in the south in full swing, another offensive was launched, against Army Group North. It had two prime objectives, one to lift the siege of Leningrad, the other to prevent Army Group South being reinforced. Leningrad and Volkhov Fronts, part of 2nd Baltic Front, and the Baltic Fleet undertook it, with 732,500 soldiers and 89,600 sailors. It lasted until March 1, ended the siege, drove the Germans back up to 175 miles (280 km) on a 370-mile (595 km) front, and took Soviet troops into Estonia for the first time since 1941. The Germans took a heavy toll of Leningrad Front, which lost 56,564 men, 13.5 percent of all its troops engaged, but overall the losses, 76,686, were 9.3 percent.

Army Group Center was left holding a bulge that the Russians christened the "Belorussian balcony." In February the Soviet General Staff began planning to eliminate it and as much as possible of Army Group Center. While it was doing so, a third operation was mounted in the south, by 4th Ukrainian Front (General Tolbukhin), the Independent Coastal Army (General Yeremenko), 4th Air Army, the Black Sea Fleet, and the Azov Flotilla, against German XVII Army in the Crimea. This involved "only" 30 divisions, one corps, and five brigades, but cleared a potential threat to

the coastal flank of the Soviet advance, and recaptured the Black Sea Fleet's main base of Sevastopol. XVII Army made a spirited defense there, but Soviet losses, at 17,754, were only 3.8 percent of the troops committed.

Preparations for assaulting the "balcony" went on under the usual heavy security. The Red Army hoodwinked the Germans into expecting the main offensive in the north and south, not the center, as successfully as the Anglo-Americans deceived them into expecting the invasion in the Pas de Calais, not Normandy. Units' radio stations closed down and reopened further south or north, transmitting fake messages from fake camps, gun and tank parks, protected by aircraft and anti-aircraft gun crews instructed to make life dangerous but not impossible for German reconnaissance aircraft. "Foreign Armies East" predicted a quiet summer for Army Group Center, and such reinforcements as were available were sent to Army Groups North and South (now renamed North Ukraine).

The Soviet plan, codenamed "Bagration," was for a sequence of up to four offensives, the last two dependent on the success of the first two. The first, which opened on June 10, involved parts of Leningrad and Karelian Fronts, aiming first to lure German forces away from the "balcony," and second to coerce Finland into surrender. The second, main offensive was by 1st Baltic, 1st, 2nd, and 3rd Belorussian Fronts, against Army Group Center (Field Marshal Busch) north and south of Minsk. If it developed satisfactorily, 1st Ukrainian Front (Marshal Konev) would advance into Poland, 2nd (General Malinovsky) and 3rd (General Tolbukhin) Ukrainian Fronts into Romania, to force its surrender and seize the Axis's only major oil fields, at Ploesti. Stalin again took a codename from Russia's past, Bagration – a Georgian, like himself, a prince and a general in the Russian army, killed fighting Napoleon in 1812.

The Anglo–American–Canadian landings in Normandy on June 6 forced considerable movement of German forces to the west. This somewhat eased the Red Army's task, but 228 Axis divisions remained on the Eastern Front, versus 58 in western Europe, though most Eastern Front divisions were well below strength. Developments in France would take more divisions westward, and the Luftwaffe's capacity to challenge Soviet air superiority was inhibited by the need to counter Anglo-American bombing. This absorbed over one-third of its aircraft and an even higher share of gun production, and Germany's overstretching left Air Fleet VI, supporting Army Group Center, with only 40 serviceable aircraft facing 7,000 Soviet.

Partisans again made a formidable contribution. On June 19 they began a seven-day rampage in Belorussia against Army Group Center's communications and supply lines. They blew up almost 1,100 rail and road bridges, derailed many trains, and destroyed or damaged thousands of locomotives and goods wagons. On June 21 Air Force bombers joined in the destruction, and on the 23rd the infantry advanced behind rolling artillery barrages from 31,000 guns, ranged almost wheel-to-wheel at an average 270 guns or Katyushas per mile (1.6 km) of front.

Against 168 divisions, 12 tank corps, and 20 brigades, Army Group Center, with only two Panzer and 36 infantry divisions, could expect hard times. Hitler made them even harder, by ordering numerous towns and cities to be made *Festungen* (fortresses), or breakwaters against the Soviet tide. But the tide simply bypassed them, and all he achieved was to make potentially mobile forces static. An example of this was III Panzer Army (General Reinhardt). Despite its title it had no tanks, only a brigade of assault guns and a battalion of "Hornet" 88mm tank-destroyers, plus 11 infantry divisions. This was little enough to face a tank corps and 24 infantry divisions of Bagramyan's 1st Baltic Front, and another tank corps and 11 infantry divisions from Chernyakhovsky's 3rd Belorussian. Yet Hitler ordered four divisions committed to the "fortress" of Vitebsk.

On June 23, the first day of "Bagration," 1st Baltic advanced 10 miles (16 km) on a 35-mile (56 km) front, and that evening Reinhardt sought Busch's permission to evacuate Vitebsk immediately. Busch refused, so on the next day Reinhardt telephoned Zeitzler, who was with Hitler at his Bavarian mountain retreat. Zeitzler consulted Hitler, who insisted Vitebsk be held. A few minutes later Reinhardt heard by radio from Vitebsk that the road west was under threat, so he repeated his request to Busch, who at once transmitted it to Hitler. He again refused, but two hours later authorized withdrawal, provided one division stayed behind.

Reinhardt thought that a pointless sacrifice, but to save the other three divisions accepted it, and at once ordered their commander, General Gollwitzer, to bring them out. But by the next day, June 25, 3rd Belorussian Front forces had met 1st Baltic, encircling Vitebsk. Of Gollwitzer's 35,000 men, only 10,000 survived to surrender; Hitler's obsession had deprived Reinhardt of one-third of his already vastly outnumbered force.

On June 24, 1st Belorussian Front (Marshal Rokossovsky), with six tank corps, 77 infantry, and nine cavalry divisions, began its offensive. By June 27 it had encircled Bobruisk and most of German IX Army (General Jordan), and jointly with 2nd Belorussian (General Zakharov) was about to encircle Mogilev and most of German IV Army (General von Tippelskirch). Only rapid withdrawals could now save Army Group Center, but Hitler still refused them, invoking the bad impression they would make on Germany's allies, particularly the Finns. He reluctantly allowed Busch to try to extricate IV and IX Armies, but drew a line on the map, and ordered Busch to hold it. By June 28 Soviet forces were already through it, so he dismissed Busch and put Army Group Center under Field Marshal Model, already commanding Army Group North Ukraine.

At the northern end of the line, Army Group North was being hard pressed by 1st Baltic Front, and the Soviet advance south of it threatened its flank. Its commander, Colonel-General Lindemann, sought permission to retreat to a shorter and more defensible line; Hitler dismissed him, and replaced him with General Friessner.

Minsk fell on July 4; most of IV and IX Armies, about 100,000 in all, were trapped east of it, and were destroyed over the next seven days. The 57,000 captured were paraded through Moscow on July 17, symbolically followed by street-cleaning vehicles. About 28 of Army Group Center's 38 divisions had been destroyed, and their losses, about 300,000 so far, ranked Bagration with Kursk. Of Army Group Center's four armies, IV and IX had been smashed, as had nine of III Panzer's 11 divisions. II Army (General Weiss) remained relatively intact, but between it and the remnants of III Panzer was a 250-mile (400 km) gap, defended only by scratch formations of border guards and training units rushed from East Prussia.

Soviet exploitation of this was rapid. 1st Baltic Front advanced north of Vilnius, capital of Lithuania. 3rd Belorussian Front took Vilnius on July 13, and pushed what was left of III Panzer Army away northwestward. 2nd Belorussian advanced 160 miles (255 km) in 10 days, to within 50 miles (80 km) of the East Prussian border, while 1st Belorussian pushed across Poland to the Vistula. Between July 28 and August 2 it secured bridgeheads at Magnuszew and Pulawy, and at the end of July it was approaching Warsaw.

The Polish Home Army, loyal to the government-in-exile in London, began the Warsaw Rising on August 1, when noise of gunfire from the east suggested that Soviet troops would soon arrive. Marshal Rokossovsky, 1st Belorussian Front's commander, was not notified beforehand, and Stalin, who intended power to pass to the Communist "Polish National Committee," denounced the rising as an attempt to improve the London government's position by seizing Warsaw before the Red Army arrived.

Militarily, 1st Belorussian Front had good reason to stop at the Vistula. It had been attacking for two months, had advanced

nearly 400 miles (640 km), suffered 28 percent casualties in dead or wounded, and outrun its supply lines. Its task, which it had fulfilled precisely, was to seize some bridgeheads, then stop to regroup and resupply. It was not required to try to seize Warsaw off the march, and at the end of July it was forced back 15–20 miles (24–32 km). But for politics, Home Army commander General Bor-Komorowski would probably have told Rokossovsky what he intended, and been advised to wait until 1st Belorussian Front, including its Soviet-equipped Polish 1st Army, could resupply and attack in support.

On August 3 the guns in the east fell silent. Thereafter the Home Army fought alone against German forces amply provided with heavy weapons, tanks, and air support. It was squeezed into smaller and smaller areas, and in the rising's sixth week Bor was

Improvisation – Soviet infantry crossing the River Dvina in Operation Bagration. (IWM NYP 31136 PR2)

authorized to seek German terms for surrender. Talks mediated by the Polish Red Cross secured a brief cease-fire on September 8 and 9, but went no further, because on September 10 1st Belorussian Front at last moved. Over the next five days Soviet and Polish 1st Army troops eliminated the Germans' east-bank bridgehead in Praga and occupied the entire east bank. But on the 11th, the newly arrived 25th Panzer Division set about pushing the Home Army away from the west bank. Polish 1st Army units attempted to cross on the nights of September 16 and 17, but those that survived the crossing were cut to pieces by German fire, and no more attempts were made.

Roosevelt's and Churchill's requests to Stalin brought on August 16 only a denunciation of the rising as "a reckless, appalling adventure" from which the Soviet command "must dissociate itself." They then attempted to supply the insurgents from the air, and sought Stalin's permission for the aircraft to fly on to Soviet-controlled airfields to refuel. Stalin initially refused, and the need to carry enough fuel for the return trip severely limited the payloads. Furthermore, lack of Soviet air support over Warsaw compelled the aircraft to drop their loads from a great height; most of them fell into the river or German hands. Only on September 10 did Stalin relent. A supply flight by 110 American bombers was mounted, but by then the Home Army held so little ground that only 30 percent of the supplies reached them. From September 13 the Soviet air force also began dropping supplies, but too late to be of use. The rising ended in a negotiated surrender on October 2.

After 68 days "Bagration" officially ended on August 29. On a front of almost 700 miles (1,125 km), Soviet forces had advanced

Troops of Polish First Army, 1st Belorussian Front, back on Polish soil. (AKG Berlin)

340–75 miles (545–600 km), at higher rates of advance than before. At Moscow in 1941 their best had been 3.7 miles (6 km) a day, at Stalingrad 2.8 miles (4.5 km), at Kursk 6.2 miles (10 km). In "Bagration" they reached 15.6 miles (25 km) in the first phase, and 8.75 miles (14 km) in the second. The cost in lives, 180,040, was 7.7 percent of the 2,411,600 committed, the same as in the Kursk offensive, much less than the 13.5 percent of Stalingrad, and for much larger gains than in either.

Since this offensive developed well, Konev's 1st Ukrainian Front was launched into the next, the Lvov–Sandomierz operation against Army Group North Ukraine, on July 13. This also ended on August 29, as successfully as the first. Konev's troops crossed the Vistula at Sandomierz, and established a large bridgehead to serve as the launching point for the next advance, into

Silesia. Reflecting the relative weakness of Army Group North Ukraine, the average daily rate of advance (up to 40 miles, or 65 km) was even higher, and losses (6.5 percent) lower, than in "Bagration" proper.

The fourth offensive, against Army Group South Ukraine and Romania, was initiated by 2nd and 3rd Ukrainian Fronts on August 20. It too ended officially on August 29, after only 10 days. The frontage of assault was about 315 miles (505 km), depth of advance ranged from 185 to 200 miles (300 to 320 km); the daily advance averaged up to 15.5 miles (25 km) for the marching infantry, and 20 miles (32 km) for the mobile forces. Losses (13,197) were only 1 percent of the 1.3 million troops involved, but militarily the victory was only partial; Army Group South Ukraine had to retreat, but Manstein frustrated Zhukov's plan to encircle and destroy it. Politically, however, the brief campaign was a triumph. With help from anti-German Romanians, 2nd Ukrainian Front occupied Ploesti on August 30, and entered

Soviet troops land on the Finnish coast. (AKG Berlin)

Bucharest on the 31st. On September 12 at Moscow Romania signed an armistice, and undertook to provide at least 12 infantry divisions to fight the Germans.

Germany's Balkans problems next involved Bulgaria, which had joined the Axis in 1941, but had not declared war on the Soviet Union. On August 26, as 3rd Ukrainian Front approached, it restated its neutrality, ordered the disarming of German troops retreating from Romania, and asked the USA and Great Britain for armistice terms. On September 5 the Soviet Union declared war, and 3rd Ukrainian Front invaded. It met no resistance, a new Bulgarian government declared war on Germany on September 9, and a Bulgarian army joined the Soviet push into Yugoslavia.

The unsuccessful July 20 coup against Hitler had been suppressed too quickly to affect Germany's war effort immediately. But Germany's allies were now falling away one after another. The liberation of Paris on August 25 was followed the next day by the flight of the collaborationist Vichy government. On August 29 a national uprising began in the puppet state of Slovakia. German troops had to be rushed there, and the rising was not suppressed until the end of October.

On September 2 Finland accepted Soviet armistice terms and on the 4th it broke off relations with Germany and announced a cease-fire. Its armistice agreement, signed in Moscow on September 19, included an undertaking to disarm any Germans still on its territory. German forces in southern Finland left quickly, but XX Mountain Army in the north formed defensive fronts on the east against the Soviets and on the south against the Finns. Marshal Meretskov sent troops and marines into action on October 7, and by the 15th the Germans were retreating into Norway. On October 25 Soviet troops liberated Kirkenes, and on the 29th reached Neiden, where they stopped. Stalin sent Meretskov, the first front commander to work himself out of a job, to take leave, then undertake a new assignment. He would command a front in the war against Japan, which Stalin had committed the Soviet Union to enter within three months of Germany's surrender.

The lull following completion of "Bagration" on August 29 was very brief. With Anglo-American forces approaching Germany's western borders, advancing in Italy and, on June 15, landing in southern France, Germany

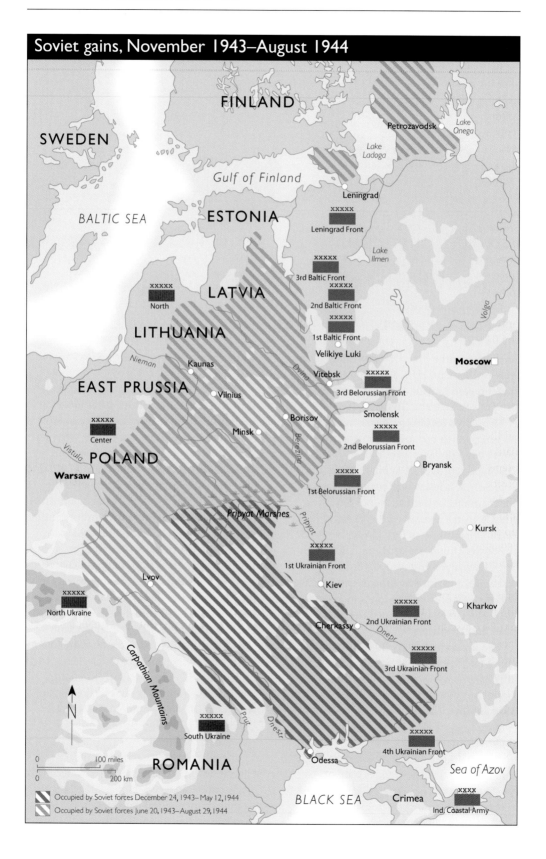

Soviet gains, November 1943–August 1944

SWEDEN

FINLAND

Petrozavodsk   Lake Onega

Lake Ladoga

Gulf of Finland

BALTIC SEA

ESTONIA

Leningrad

xxxxx
Leningrad Front

Lake Ilmen

xxxxx
North

LATVIA

xxxxx
3rd Baltic Front

xxxxx
2nd Baltic Front

xxxxx
1st Baltic Front

Volga

LITHUANIA

Velikiye Luki

Moscow

Nieman   Kaunas

Vitebsk

xxxxx
3rd Belorussian Front

EAST PRUSSIA   Vilnius

Dvina

Borisov

Smolensk

xxxxx
Center

Minsk

Berezina

xxxxx
2nd Belorussian Front

Vistula

POLAND

Bryansk

Warsaw

xxxxx
1st Belorussian Front

Pripyat Marshes

Pripyat

Kursk

xxxxx
1st Ukrainian Front

xxxxx
North Ukraine

Lvov

Kiev

Kharkov

xxxxx
2nd Ukrainian Front

Cherkassy

Dnepr

xxxxx
3rd Ukrainian Front

Carpathian Mountains

N

xxxxx
South Ukraine

Prut   *Dnestr*

xxxxx
4th Ukrainian Front

0   100 miles
0   200 km

ROMANIA

Odessa

Sea of Azov

Occupied by Soviet forces December 24, 1943–May 12, 1944
Occupied by Soviet forces June 20, 1943–August 29, 1944

BLACK SEA   Crimea

xxxx
Ind. Coastal Army

was now fighting on four fronts. On July 31 Army Group North was briefly isolated when 1st Baltic Front reached the Gulf of Riga, but after Hitler dismissed its commander, Friessner, his successor, Schoerner, mounted a counteroffensive that by August 21 had reopened a corridor to Army Group Center. It was, however, only 12 miles (19 km) wide, and Stavka made its closure high priority in a campaign to isolate and if possible destroy Army Group North. The Baltic Fleet and five fronts (Leningrad, 1st, 2nd, and 3rd Baltic, 3rd Belorussian) took part. With 1,546,400 men in 156 divisions and 11 brigades, they outnumbered Army Group North by about three to one in manpower and more than that in weapons.

The offensive began on September 14, only 16 days after the end of "Bagration." In the first three days, 1st Baltic Front advanced 30 miles (48 km), to within 16 miles (26 km) of Riga, but strong German defense made the progress of 2nd and 3rd Baltic Fronts painfully slow. However, Leningrad Front joined in on September 17, captured Tallin on the 22nd, then turned south on to the flanks of XVI and XVIII Armies, which were preparing to withdraw from Narva to positions north of Riga. Also on the 22nd, 2nd and 3rd Baltic Fronts broke through, and by the 27th they were northeast of Riga, up against the northern section of the "Sigulda Line," which ran in a semicircle around Riga at 25–30 miles (40–48 km) from it. The 31 German divisions manning the line beat off attempts to break through off the march, so the two fronts regrouped for a set-piece assault. An attempt by 1st Baltic to break through from the south also failed, and Stavka ordered it instead to head for the Lithuanian port of Memel. It moved on

OPPOSITE: In this period the battle for the Dnepr (August–December 1943) was followed by the lifting of the siege of Leningrad (January 1944), and by Operation Bagration in Belorussia (June–August 1944), with associated offensives on the Finnish, Carpathian, and southern sectors. By the end of August, the Germans had been expelled from almost all Soviet territory, and the Red Army had entered Romania, Poland, and East Prussia.

October 5, and reached the coast at Palanga, north of Memel, five days later.

Memel would not fall until January 1945, but by the end of October 1st Baltic had isolated most of Army Group North in the Kurland peninsula. 3rd Baltic had also reached the coast, south of Memel, and was in East Prussia, only 60 miles (100 km) from its capital, Koenigsberg. Leningrad and 3rd Baltic Fronts swept the Germans out of Estonia, and all five fronts except 3rd Belorussian were along the Sigulda Line by the beginning of October.

Schoerner, although appointed to "Stand Fast," soon realized that Army Group North would be cut off if it did not withdraw into East Prussia. In early September he sought Hitler's permission to do so, but by the time Hitler gave it, in mid-September, the Red Army had made it impossible.

In all campaigns from September 1944 onward, German mobility was very low for lack of fuel. Loss of the Ploesti oil fields, and Anglo-American air attacks on the hydrogenation plants that manufactured oil from coal, reduced German petrol production in September to only 8 percent of its April level. In 1941 the Wehrmacht had been more mobile than the Red Army, but by 1944 the reverse was true. The Red Army, with its indigenous oil supplies and fleets of US-made trucks, could move and supply its troops far faster than the German – and do so in safety, as fuel shortages kept most of the Luftwaffe on the ground.

Coincident with the Baltic operation (September 14–November 24) were offensives in the eastern Carpathians (September 8– 28 October) by 1st and 4th Ukrainian Fronts, and Yugoslavia (September 28– October 20) and Hungary (October 29– February 13, 1945) by 2nd and 3rd Ukrainian Fronts. The forces involved in the simultaneous September–October 1944 offensives were 295 divisions and 26 brigades, more than Germany's entire Western and Eastern Front forces, nominally 276 divisions, but many now divisions only in name.

Hungary was the next German ally to come under the Soviet sledgehammer. Its ruler, Admiral Horthy, sent emissaries to Moscow on October 1 to seek an armistice, but the Germans learned of this and seized all Hungary's main communications centers. On October 15, Horthy broadcast that Hungary's war was over, but a German-supported coup installed a pro-Nazi government. It ordered the armed forces to fight on, but in Hungary, as elsewhere, enthusiasm to die for a lost cause was waning, and mass desertions began. About the only reason to continue fighting was knowledge of the atrocities committed by Soviet troops on captured territory, of which the Germans became aware when they recaptured Nyiregyhaza after a week of Soviet occupation.

Despite three years of bombing German civilians, the Anglo-Americans proclaimed that their war was against Nazism, not the German people. With some exceptions, German occupying forces behaved reasonably toward non-resistant civilians in western Europe, and in general treated their captured soldiers in accordance with the Geneva Convention.

But Nazism defined Slavs as racial inferiors, destined for an only slightly better fate than the genocide prepared for the Jews. Soviet troops on recaptured territory had their indoctrination in hatred reinforced by German atrocities. Many saw these for themselves and the rest were told about them; villages burned, their inhabitants killed, public hangings and, in Belorussia and eastern Poland, a succession of extermination camps.

When they entered hostile territory they responded in kind, with murder, mutilation, rape, and looting, not always bothering to distinguish between allies and enemies. The Soviet government did not officially sanction this, but did nothing to stop it until it threatened discipline. When a Yugoslav partisan leader, Milovan Djilas, complained to Stalin about Soviet raping of Yugoslav women, Stalin dismissed it with "What's so awful about having fun with a woman?" A ruler capable of deporting entire peoples as potential or actual collaborators with the Germans – Volga Germans, Crimean Tatars, Chechens, Ingush, Balkars, Kalmyks, Meskhetians – was hardly likely to be squeamish about his troops' behavior. About all that can be said in mitigation is that mass atrocities were short-lived, not genocidal, and not followed up, as in the German occupation, by mass killings. However, counterparts to the Gestapo, the NKVD (People's Commissariat for Internal Affairs) and SMERSH ("Death to Spies") teams conducted more selective, but still large-scale, shootings and deportations. Not until April 20, 1945, did Stalin order that Soviet troops' attitude to the German people "must now change."

Fear of what lay in store prompted Axis forces to fight on desperately in the east, while the will to do so in the west began to evaporate. Guderian even proposed making peace with the Anglo-Americans while continuing to fight the Soviets, but Hitler would not hear of it. His riposte was instead to try to repeat the decisive breakthrough of 1940 in the Ardennes, demanding at the same time house-by-house defense of Budapest and an offensive in the Lake Balaton area of Hungary, west of the Danube.

1945

The Ardennes offensive, begun on December 16, 1944, was initially successful enough to prompt Churchill on January 6 to ask Stalin to attack to draw German forces away. Stalin advanced by eight days the Vistula–Oder operation, planned to begin on the 20th. Some Soviet historians thereafter claimed that this saved the Allies from defeat, but the Americans had turned the tide even before Churchill's request.

On January 12 1st Belorussian and 1st Ukrainian Fronts attacked, supported by the adjacent wings of 2nd Belorussian and 4th Ukrainian; on the next day, 4th and 2nd Ukrainian Fronts attacked in the western Carpathians, and 2nd and 3rd Belorussian in East Prussia. Altogether, in two days, 436 divisions, 30 corps, and 31 brigades, with almost 4.5 million men, went into action. Many formations were understrength, but that was even truer of their opponents. German infantry divisions no longer had nine battalions; existing ones had six, some new ones only four. Panzer divisions, of 400 tanks each in 1940, now averaged fewer than 100.

The main Soviet blow would fall on the 70 understrength divisions of Army Groups Center and "A," against which 1st Belorussian and 1st Ukrainian Fronts, including Polish 1st Army, deployed 181 divisions and 14 brigades.

At the start of 1945 Germany's Eastern Front comprised five Army Groups, from north to south:

North (XVI and XVIII Armies). Isolated in
   Kurland.
Center (III Panzer, IV and II Armies). Eastern
   Prussia and northern Poland.
A (IX and IV Panzer, XVII and I Panzer
   Armies). Southern Poland–northern
   Carpathians.
South (VI and VIII German; I, II, and
   III Hungarian). Hungary.
F (II Panzer). Hungary and Yugoslavia.

On January 26, Army Group North was renamed Army Group Kurland, Center was renamed North, and A became Center.

The largest Soviet offensive, against the renamed Army Groups Center (Reinhardt) and North (Schoerner), would set the stage for the final advance to Berlin. It was launched from three bridgeheads across the Vistula: 1st Belorussian Front's at Magnuszew and Pulawy, and 1st Ukrainian's at Baranow. Both fronts were to advance to the Oder and seize bridgeheads across it, only about 60 miles (100 km) from Berlin. Stalin abolished the posts of Stavka representatives; Zhukov, remaining Deputy Supreme Commander, took command of 1st Belorussian Front from Rokossovsky, who moved to 2nd Belorussian Front, tasked to envelope the Germans in East Prussia and protect Zhukov's northern flank. Konev retained command of 1st Ukrainian Front; it was to advance into Silesia, and Stalin

instructed Konev to keep destruction there to the minimum.

Poland was to be moved bodily westward, ceding territory in the east and receiving compensation at Germany's expense, including Silesia. Stalin wanted Poland to receive Silesia's industries as intact as possible, to mollify resentment over the cessions in the east. Konev achieved this by advancing one of his tank armies north, and the other south of Silesia, compelling IV Panzer Army to withdraw too hastily to do much demolition. Red Army mobility now so outclassed German that in the 23 days of the Vistula–Oder operation, even its infantry advanced on average 12–14 miles (19–22 km) a day, taking major cities such as Warsaw, Poznan, Lodz, and Breslau while doing so; and "irrevocable" losses were low, 43,476 (just under 2 percent) of the 2.2 million deployed.

Of the two offensives launched on January 13, the East Prussian, by 2nd and 3rd Belorussian Fronts and one army of 1st Baltic, was much the larger, involving 1.67 million men, in 157 divisions and 10 brigades. Army Group North resisted much more determinedly than Army Group Center; the Soviet rate of advance over the operation's 103 days averaged only about 1.25 miles (2 km) a day, and "irrevocable" losses, at 126,464 (7.6 percent), were proportionally almost four times as heavy.

The offensive by 4th and 2nd Ukrainian Fronts in the western Carpathians involved "only" 79 divisions and seven brigades. Including two Romanian armies (I and IV) and a Czechoslovak army corps, it had 593,000 men. It lasted 38 days, losses were just over 19,000 (3.2 percent), and the average daily advance, 4 miles (6.4 km), was creditable in mountainous terrain.

Next, on February 10, came an offensive in East Pomerania, by 2nd Belorussian Front, the right wing of 1st Belorussian and, from March 1, Polish First Army. That this offensive, involving 996,000 men, could be mounted while 2nd Belorussian's East Prussia operation was still in progress, and only a week after 1st Belorussian had concluded the

From the Vistula to the Oder, January 1945

POMERANIA

Stettin

Grudziadz   EAST PRUSSIA

Bydgoszcz   xxxxx

Center

REINHARDT

Berlin   Kustrin   Gniezno

Frankfurt   Poznan   POLAND   Modlin

Warsaw

Cottbus   Krotoszyn   xxxxx   Lodz

GERMANY   HARPE   Tomaszow Maz

Dresden   Gorlitz   Namslau   Warta

Breslau   Czestochowa   Kielce

Katowice

Prague   Biala   Tarnow

CZECHOSLOVAKIA   Nowy Sacz   Jaslow

Zakopane

xxxxx   2nd Belorussian Front (5 Armies)

ROKOSSOVSKY

xxxxx   1st Belorussian Front (8 Armies)

Magnuszew   ZHUKOV

Pulawy   Lublin

Jozelow

Sandomierz   xxxxx   1st Ukranian Front (6 Armies)

KONEV

xxxxx   PETROV

4th Ukranian Front (3 Armies)

——— Front Line on January 11, 1945
- - - - Front Line on February 2, 1945
———— German defence lines
◄——— Soviet attacks

0   50 miles

0   100 km

This Soviet offensive lasted only 22 days (January 12–February 2, 1945), but ended with a seizure of bridgeheads across the Oder only about 60 miles (100 km) from Berlin.

Vistula–Oder offensive, testified to the now overwhelming Soviet superiority. However, it also placed very heavy demands on units worn down in previous weeks' fighting.

The operation lasted till April 4, the Soviet advance was about 85 miles (135 km), the daily rate averaging only 1.5–2 miles (2.4–3.2 km), and losses were 55,315 (5.6 percent). The opponent was the newly created Army Group Vistula, of II and IX Armies, both agglomerations of units and parts of units, and a re-formed XI Army, which lacked most of the necessities for fighting. They were commanded not by a professional soldier (Hitler increasingly distrusted them for recommending withdrawals, or even surrender), but by Heinrich Himmler, head of the SS and police.

Army Group Vistula was inserted north of Army Group Center, and these two were to cover Germany's eastern approaches, while Army Group South in Hungary, the forces in Italy, and Army Group E (withdrawn from Greece to Yugoslavia) covered the south and southeast. Hitler and Himmler were now so divorced from reality as to expect a counteroffensive by Army Group Vistula to decide the entire war in Germany's favor. It began on February 16, and pushed 1st Belorussian Front back about 7 miles (11 km), but by the 20th it had been stopped, and the six divisions that conducted it were counterattacked on March 1 by six armies. Some units held out until the war ended, but others fled in panic, and as an organized entity Army Group Vistula ceased to exist.

A competent professional, Colonel-General Heinrici, replaced Himmler on March 20, but there was little left for him to command. Gdynia fell on March 28, and Danzig on the 30th. The Soviets claimed

91,000 prisoners; the operation removed any risk of a flank attack on 1st Belorussian Front's planned drive to Berlin, and freed 10 more armies for that drive.

While 1st Belorussian and 1st Ukrainian Fronts were gathering for the final lunge to Berlin, Hitler ordered an offensive in Hungary, aimed at recapturing Budapest and safeguarding the minor oil-producing districts in Hungary and Austria. VI SS Panzer Army, attacking from east of Lake Balaton, was to spearhead it, while VI Army and a Hungarian corps pushed south on its left, II Panzer Army attacked due east between Balaton and the Drava River, and Army Group E attacked the I Bulgarian and III Yugoslav Armies, guarding 3rd Ukrainian Front's left flank.

Young soldiers being trained how to use a Panzerfaust (anti-tank gun), 1945. (AKG Berlin)

Marshal Tolbukhin knew an offensive was imminent, and Stavka had already approved a defensive battle followed by a counteroffensive. Army Group E and II Panzer Army attacked on the night of March 5. The main assault, by VI SS Panzer and VI Armies, went in the next morning, and made 16 miles (26 km) in four days, but it was then halted by 3rd Ukrainian's massed artillery and infantry. Casualties on both sides were heavy, but by March 15 the offensive had clearly lost its impetus, so Stavka ordered the counteroffensive to start on the 16th.

On that day 3rd Ukrainian Front (including I Bulgarian Army), part of 2nd Ukrainian Front, and the Soviet navy's Danube Flotilla began the Vienna Strategic Offensive, involving 644,700 Soviet and 100,900 Bulgarian troops, in 85 divisions and three brigades. Expulsion of the Germans from Hungary forced Army Group E to begin withdrawing from Yugoslavia. Soviet forces, advancing into eastern Austria and southern Czechoslovakia, took Vienna on April 13. The operation formally concluded on April 15, and on the next day 1st Belorussian (Zhukov), 2nd Belorussian (Rokossovsky), and 1st Ukrainian (Konev) Fronts, and the Polish First and Second Armies, began the final push to Berlin.

For this they massed 1.9 million Soviet and 156,000 Polish troops, in 234 divisions and 16 brigades, with 41,000 guns and mortars, 6,200 tanks and assault guns, and 7,500 aircraft. Against them were Army Group Vistula (Heinrici), with two armies, III Panzer (von Manteuffel) and IX (Busse), while IV Panzer Army (Graeser) of Army Group Center faced Konev's troops across the Neisse river. These three armies had between them 39 divisions; despite their titles the two Panzer armies had only one Panzer division each, the same as IX Army, and there were three Panzer and three Panzer Grenadier divisions in reserve.

With forces from elsewhere committed during the battle, the Germans fielded about 50 divisions, and perhaps as many as 100 battalions of the Volkssturm. This, a barely trained "people's militia," was under Nazi Party, not army control, and equipped mostly with obsolete German or captured weapons, though a few had the formidable anti-tank Panzerfaust. Some police units and Hitler Youth detachments also took part. Luftwaffe support comprised only about 300 serviceable aircraft.

Zhukov planned to pulverize the forward defenses with a 30-minute artillery and air bombardment, then send in the infantry, turning night into day and blinding the defenders with 143 searchlights, and expected to cover the 60-odd miles (100 km) to Berlin in 11 days. This assumed that, as in previous offensives, the tanks would reach open country once the defenses were penetrated. However, the plan proved over-optimistic because both the terrain and the intensity of the defense differed from previous campaigns. The ground was criss-crossed by streams, canals, and channels of the Oder, and was soggy. There were up to nine lines of defenses, and German positions on the Seelow heights overlooked the whole area.

Meanwhile, Anglo-American forces were also pushing into Germany, and Churchill and Field Marshal Montgomery favored trying to take Berlin before the Red Army. Eisenhower, however, believed (wrongly) that Hitler would continue the war from an "Alpine Redoubt" in southern Bavaria, western Austria, and Czechoslovakia. He therefore directed one of his three US armies to advance to meet Soviet forces at the Elbe, and directed the other two toward the putative "Redoubt." On March 28 he informed Stalin of his intentions. Stalin replied immediately, declaring Berlin strategically unimportant, and lying that his main thrust would be toward Leipzig and Dresden. Then he summoned Zhukov and Konev to Moscow.

When they arrived, appropriately on April 1, he lied to them that the Allies were planning a rapier-thrust to take Berlin before the Red Army, and told them to be ready to go on April 16. Zhukov's 1st Belorussian Front would attack directly westward, with Konev's supporting him from the south and also driving toward Leipzig and Dresden, as he had told Eisenhower it would. Rokossovsky was to protect Zhukov's northern flank by taking Stettin and driving toward Schleswig-Holstein. To exploit the rivalry between Zhukov and Konev, Stalin mapped the demarcation line between them only as far as Luebben, about 50 miles (80 km) southeast of Berlin. The implication was that if Konev reached its end first, he could turn north.

Zhukov attacked before dawn on April 16. After the barrage, the searchlights were turned on. However, the smoke and dust raised by the barrage reflected the light into the faces of his infantry, blinding them where not silhouetting them as targets. IX Army had good defensive positions, particularly on the Seelow heights, and the troops, to stiffen their will, had been told that anyone retreating without orders would immediately be shot.

The Soviet infantry's progress was so slow and costly that around noon Zhukov abandoned normal Soviet practice of committing the tanks only after the infantry had made a breach, and ordered his two tank armies to make the breach themselves. The few roads were crowded with men and vehicles, slowing the tanks' progress and making all easy targets, especially for the 88mm guns behind and above the anti-tank ditches. Not until late on April 17 was the first line of the Seelow defenses breached, and it took another day to breach the second. After four days Zhukov was two days behind schedule, so Stalin authorized Konev to break into Berlin from the south.

Konev's assault had gone far better, despite having to cross the Neisse River, with easier terrain, sandy soil, and less waterlogging. He innovated with smokescreens, not searchlights, and more successfully, though some cynical old

Soviet tanks in central Berlin. (AKG Berlin)

The Battle of Berlin, April 1945

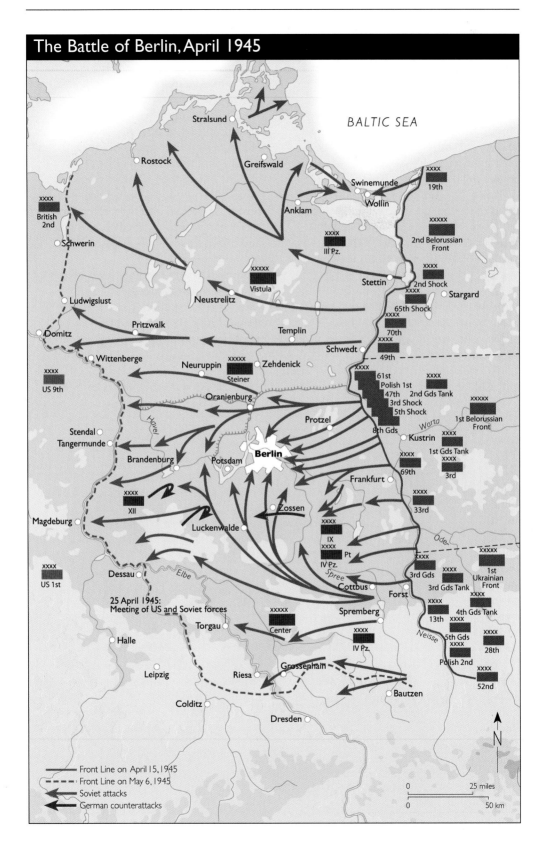

BALTIC SEA

Stralsund

Rostock

Greifswald

Swinemunde

XXXX
19th

Wollin

Anklam

XXXX
British
2nd

Schwerin

XXXX
III Pz.

Stettin

XXXXX
2nd Belorussian
Front

XXXX
2nd Shock

XXXXX
Vistula

Stargard

XXXX
65th Shock

Ludwigslust

Neustrelitz

XXXX
70th

Pritzwalk

Templin

XXXX
49th

Domitz

Wittenberge

Schwedt

Neuruppin

XXXXX
Steiner

Zehdenick

XXXX
US 9th

XXXX
61st
Polish 1st
47th   2nd Gds Tank
3rd Shock
5th Shock

XXXXX
1st Belorussian
Front

Oranienburg

Protzel

Warta

Stendal

Havel

8th Gds

Kustrin

Tangermunde

Brandenburg

Potsdam

Berlin

XXXX
1st Gds Tank

XXXX
69th

XXXX
3rd

Frankfurt

XXXX
XII

Zossen

XXXX
33rd

Magdeburg

Luckenwalde

XXXX
IX
XXXX
IV Pz.

Pt

XXXX
US 1st

Dessau

Elbe

Spree

Cottbus

Forst

XXXX
3rd Gds

XXXX
3rd Gds Tank

XXXXX
1st
Ukrainian
Front

Ode

XXXXX

25 April 1945:
Meeting of US and Soviet forces

Torgau

XXXXX
Center

Spremberg

XXXX
13th

XXXX
4th Gds Tank

Halle

XXXX
IV Pz.

Neisse

XXXX
5th Gds

XXXX
28th

Leipzig

Riesa

Grossenhain

Polish 2nd

XXXX
52nd

Colditz

Bautzen

Dresden

N

Front Line on April 15, 1945
Front Line on May 6, 1945
Soviet attacks
German counterattacks

0   25 miles

0   50 km

Soviet soldiers hoisting the Red Flag over the Reichstag.
(AKG Berlin)

soldiers would later say, "Maybe they
blinded the Germans, they certainly blinded
us." His engineer troops performed near-
miracles, setting up many bridges or ferries
within a few hours. Both his tank armies
were across the river by April 17, and on the
next day they reached two of the "fortress
towns," Cottbus and Spremberg. The tanks
bypassed both, advancing north and south
of Spremberg, and driving a wedge between
Army Groups Vistula and Center.

Toward nightfall on April 19, 2nd Tank
Army of Zhukov's Front at last reached open
country and Berlin's northeast outskirts,
cutting between III Panzer and IX Armies,
and continuing westwards toward the Elbe.
On the 20th, Chuykov's 8th Guards Army
reached the eastern outskirts and, reverting
to his Stalingrad tactics, began expelling the
defenders almost building by building.
Zhukov's determination not to be outpaced
by Konev led him to do what Chuykov had

sedulously avoided, namely send massed
tanks into street battles, where Panzerfausts
knocked out many of them. Hasty
improvisation with sheet metal and
sandbags provided the tanks with extra
protection, but the numerous canals and
rivers in the city impeded progress until
assault engineers braved intense fire to
lay pontoon bridges.

Early on April 25 Chuykov's men reached
Schoenefeld airfield, only to find Rybalko's
3rd Guards Tank Army of 1st Ukrainian
already there. They had advanced 60 miles
(100 km) in two days, overrunning OKH's
headquarters at Zossen on the way, and
thereby ruining the defense's prospects of
coordination. On April 25 Konev ordered a
northward offensive across the city center to
take the Tiergarten and Reichstag. But when
General Rybalko reached the Landwehr
Canal, only 300 yds (275 m) from the
Reichstag, he found Chuykov there, and
Zhukov, furious at his presence. Konev had
to turn Rybalko westward and leave the
Reichstag to Zhukov and Chuykov. Konev

was naturally disappointed, Rybalko even more so, but there was some poetic justice in Stalin's decision to have the Reichstag and nearby Chancellery, with Hitler's bunker, taken by the defenders of Leningrad, Moscow, and Stalingrad.

On April 29 8th Guards Army began storming the Tiergarten from the south, while 3rd Shock Army (Colonel-General V. I. Kuznetsov) attacked from the north. Only

Soviet troops celebrating the capture of the Reichstag. (AKG Berlin)

¼ mile (0.4 km) separated them, but it was cluttered with large buildings and strongly defended. The Reichstag had to be taken room by room, and Kuznetsov's men got there first. They broke in just after 1:00 am on April 30, and 10 hours later a Red Banner appeared on the roof.

On that day Hitler committed suicide, and that evening the Germans requested negotiations. At 3:30 am on May 1, Colonel-General Hans Krebs, Chief of General Staff of OKH, arrived at Chuykov's headquarters to report Hitler's death and seek armistice

terms. Chuykov telephoned Zhukov, who insisted on unconditional surrender, telephoned Moscow, and had Stalin woken to receive the news. He endorsed Zhukov's demand and went back to sleep. Krebs held out for negotiations with the new government of Admiral Dönitz, returned to his headquarters, and at 4:00 am sent a written refusal to surrender, whereupon the Soviet offensive resumed. Early on May 2 the garrison commander, General Weidling, notified Chuykov that he wished to surrender, and firing ceased at 6:00 am.

The surrender applied only to Berlin; elsewhere fighting continued for several more days, but by May 3 Allied forces had met along the Elbe and Muelde rivers, 2nd Belorussian Front meeting the British, and 1st Belorussian the Americans. Sporadic clashes, some of them fierce, continued, but the last big Soviet action would be in Czechoslovakia.

A popular uprising began in Prague on May 5. German forces set about suppressing it, and the insurgents sought help. Their first source was an unlikely one, the 2nd Division of the turncoat Soviet General Vlasov's Russian Liberation Army (ROA), hoping to receive political asylum in Czechoslovakia or surrender to American 3rd Army, approaching from the west. Much more was needed, so Stalin directed 1st, 3rd, and 4th Ukrainian Fronts to provide it. Konev dispatched Rybalko's tanks to Prague, and on May 11 the Germans surrendered. A hard fate awaited the Russian Liberation Army. Vlasov was hanged for treason in Moscow in1946, his men faced death or long prison terms, and Soviet soldiers shot many ROA wounded in their hospital beds in Prague.

Four days earlier, on May 7, Colonel-General Jodl and Admiral von Friedeburg had signed an unconditional surrender in Reims. Although it stipulated surrender to Soviet as well as Allied forces, Stalin saw it as denigrating the Soviet contribution, and insisted on a more comprehensive official surrender ceremony in Berlin. This took place in Karlshorst on May 8, Zhukov signing for the Soviet Union.

At the victory parade in Moscow on June 24, in pouring rain, the standards of German army and Waffen SS regiments were cast at the foot of the podium where Stalin stood. But the war was not yet over.

The Allies' main reason for seeking Soviet participation against Japan was the experience in the Pacific islands and Burma that Japanese soldiers genuinely preferred death to surrender. The largest remaining Japanese force outside Japan was the Kwantung Army, believed to number over

800,000 men and deployed in Manchuria, then the Japanese puppet state of Manchukuo. The Soviet army was best located for dealing with it, and to ensure overwhelming strength Stalin supplemented the forces already there with experienced formations from Europe.

By July 31 almost 1.7 million troops were there, in 88 divisions, 34 brigades, and 21 "fortified areas" (garrison troops), with a 16,000-strong Mongolian cavalry and motorized infantry contingent. The force formed three fronts, from west to east Transbaikal (Marshal Malinovsky), 1st Far Eastern (Marshal Meretskov), and 2nd Far Eastern (Army General M. A. Purkayev), supported by the Pacific Fleet and Amur Flotilla (Admiral Yumashev).

Zhukov's first battle in command had been his defeat of the Japanese invasion of

Soviet troops indicate where Hitler's body was found. (Topham Picturepoint)

Mongolia in 1939, so he would seem a logical choice as Commander-in-Chief for the Far East campaign. But Stalin already saw Zhukov's popularity as a threat, and appointed Vasilevsky instead. The main difficulties were logistical: Transbaikal Front forces would have to cross the Gobi Desert and Great Khingan mountains, and the theater of war was very large. The four armies from Europe took no tanks because the latest three months' production was awaiting them in the Far East, bringing the total there to 5,500, all of them superior to the 1,155 lighter Japanese tanks. They also outnumbered the Japanese by almost five to one in guns (26,000 to 5,360) and over two to one in aircraft (3,900 to 1,800).

Stalin succeeded in deluding Roosevelt and Churchill into conceding a high price (the Kurile Islands, South Sakhalin, and the restoration of rights in Manchuria originally held by Tsarist Russia) for Soviet participation. In fact, he was eager to pose to

ABOVE: Turncoat General Vlasov reviewing troops of his German-equipped Russian Liberation Army. Ironically, the only action it saw was against the Germans in Prague in 1945. (AKG Berlin)

BELOW: Soviet forces (many in US-supplied trucks) enter Prague. (AKG Berlin)

the Soviet people as player of the decisive role in the defeat of Japan as well as of Germany, and the avenger of Russia's defeat by Japan in the war of 1904–05. His desire for military pre-eminence was shown at the final meetings to review the preparations for invading Manchuria. These took place in the Kremlin on July 26–27; on the first day he had the Supreme Soviet revive the rank of Generalissimus, dormant in Russia since 1800, and on the second day had it conferred upon himself.

On August 5 Vasilevsky notified him that he would be ready to attack on the 10th. But on the 6th, the first atomic bomb was dropped at Hiroshima, and it needed no military genius to realize that if the Americans had only one other bomb, they would drop it as soon as possible, to coerce Japan into surrender by giving it the impression that they had many more. Should Japan surrender before the Soviet

The Yalta Conference, February 1945. Stalin agreed to join the war against Japan within three months of victory in Europe. By the Potsdam Conference (July), the USA had a new, strongly anti-Communist president, Truman, who hoped the new atomic weapons (successfully tested on July 24) would force Japan to surrender without Soviet participation. Soviet forces entered the war just hours before the Emperor resolved to surrender. (AKG Berlin)

Union attacked, Stalin would get the territorial accessions he had sought, but by American grace and favor. It was therefore imperative to join in the war before a second bomb was dropped, so he ordered Vasilevsky to bring the attack forward to midnight on the night of August 8–9. Vasilevsky complied, and the Soviet Union entered the war just two minutes less than 12 hours before the second bomb was dropped, on Nagasaki, at two minutes before midday.

The Emperor had already decided at 7:30 that morning to tell the Supreme War

Council meeting that evening of his decision to surrender, but his decision was not made public until August 14. Despite fierce, sometimes suicidal resistance, Transbaikal Front's right wing was by then heading for Beijing, its center for Port Arthur, its left for Changchun. Two armies of 1st Far Eastern Front were converging on Tsitsihar, while 2nd Far Eastern's left wing was heading for Harbin, its center for Korea, its left into South Sakhalin and the Kurile Islands; the southernmost Kuriles were occupied on September 2, the day of the official surrender ceremony in Tokyo Bay. In his broadcast that day, Stalin referred specifically to the victory as something "the men of my generation have awaited for 40 years."

On August 15 General Yamada, commanding the Kwantung Army, heard the Emperor's broadcast announcing the surrender, but decided to await written confirmation. On the 17th a member of the royal family arrived with written orders, and Yamada complied on August 19. To seize as much territory as possible before the cease-fire, Vasilevsky sent improvised airborne units to Manchuria's main cities – Mukden, Harbin, Changchun, Kirin, and Port Arthur – to hold the airports and communications centers pending the ground forces' arrival. On the 23rd Stalin proclaimed the victorious end of the campaign. Last to be taken were the southern Kurile Islands, occupied without resistance on September 2, the day of the official surrender ceremony in Tokyo Bay.

August 19, 1945. General Yamada, Commander-in-Chief of the Japanese Kwantung Army, arrives at Marshal Vasilevsky's headquarters to sign the surrender. (Novosti [London])

ABOVE: Soviet troops parade in
Harbin. (Novosti [London])

BELOW: Japanese troops leave for Siberian prisoner-of-war camps. During the
very brief campaign 662,000 Japanese were captured, and kept at forced labor
in the Soviet Union for up to 10 years. (Novosti [London])

The campaign in the Far East, August 1945

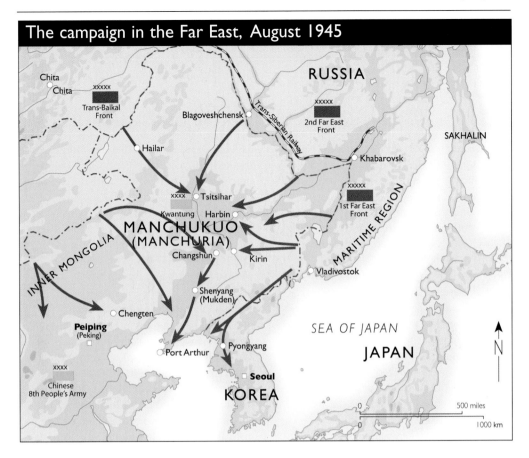

Compared to the campaigns in Europe, Soviet casualties were small: 12,031 Soviet and 72 Mongolian troops lost, 0.7 percent of those engaged. The campaign nominally lasted 25 days, but actual fighting took less than two weeks. Putting down anti-Soviet nationalist guerrillas in Ukraine and the Baltic States would take another two years, but that could mostly be left to the NKVD. The Red Army's war was over.

This campaign was noteworthy for the logistical problems of supplying a highly mechanized force, 1.7 million strong, over enormous distances. The actual fighting lasted only two weeks. For the Soviet Union's brief participation, Stalin took more Japanese territory (Southern Sakhalin and the Kurile Islands) than his allies, who had fought Japan for several years.

The German and the Russian view

Few German soldiers were committed Nazis, but all took into the invasion a faith in Hitler and his generals created by two years of victories, and the younger ones several years of indoctrination in school and the Hitler Youth about German racial superiority. The welcome they received, particularly in Ukraine and the Baltic States, and the enormous early captures of Soviet troops boosted that euphoria, but it faded somewhat after weeks of tramping over seemingly endless plains, and finding that however many of the enemy they killed or captured, more came at them the next day. Panzer crews were shocked to find the newest Soviet tank, the T-34, superior to their hitherto unstoppable Marks III and IV, but in 1941 there were few of them.

The defeat at Moscow affected morale little; they attributed it more to the weather than to the enemy, and expected to reassert their superiority when summer came. This they duly did, only to suffer another winter disaster at Stalingrad. This depressed them more, but Manstein's successful counteroffensive in February 1943 somewhat restored morale.

The crunch came at Kursk. The Prokhorovka tank battle was the swan song of the Panzers as attack spearheads, until the abortive Ardennes and Balaton offensives of 1945; the infantry for the first time experienced failure in summer, decisive Soviet air superiority, and the start of a series of Soviet offensives that dwarfed even that of Stalingrad. Most German soldiers remained disciplined and skillful to the end, but after Kursk they fought in fear of the consequences of defeat rather than in expectation of victory.

A typical German soldier from a tank destroyer unit, who fought in the east from the very first day, summed up his experiences as follows. First encounters with the Red Army suggested they would not be much trouble, but "things were different later." Many felt they should not have invaded, but it was not safe to say so. His belief that the war was lost came with the retreat from the Volga, but he and his comrades expected to be shot if captured, so they fought hard and nobody deserted or defected.

He had a month's home leave in mid-1942; before going on leave soldiers were sent to a transit camp for two weeks, and fed better than usual, so as to make a better impression at home. On leave they were privileged to wear civilian clothes and received extra rations of food and chocolate. He found home front propaganda so untruthful that he listened mostly to the BBC; this was punishable by imprisonment or death, but soldiers sent back to the Soviet Union thought they would probably be killed anyway, so were not deterred. He was shocked by the poor standard of replacements for casualties, and his friends envied him when a leg wound finally removed him from the front. He "would not wish his worst enemy" to have to fight the Russians.

In the Third Reich's last throes desertions increased, despite the activities of SS execution squads. So many units retreated, to surrender to the Anglo-Americans rather than the Red Army, that General Eisenhower had to threaten to close the Elbe crossings against them. Their fears were not baseless; the Anglo-Americans released most of their prisoners within two years, whereas those taken by the Soviets were kept at forced labor from four to 10 years.

The Red Army had a draconian disciplinary code together with Stalin's 1941

Order 270, which defined "voluntary surrender" (i.e., if neither wounded nor unconscious) as treason. Yet the first six months saw mass surrenders on an unprecedented scale. Since only a little over half the Soviet population was Russian, soldiers' attitudes to the war covered as wide a spectrum as the civilian populations from which they came. The instinct for self-preservation kept most in the ranks, but surrender at the first opportunity was rife in 1941, particularly among conscripts from the recently annexed Baltic States and former eastern Poland.

The backbone of the Red Army was the ethnic Russian, mostly a peasant or first-generation urban worker. He retained the hardiness and self-sacrificing qualities of his forebears, but added basic literacy and familiarity with machinery that they lacked. His training and tactics were generally primitive – right until the end of the war, infantry attacked frontally in successive waves, with little regard for casualties;

The reality of war. (AKG Berlin)

outflanking maneuvers were usually left to the tanks and motorized infantry. The heavy casualties affected morale less than they might have; they were frequent enough to become regarded as normal, and the soldiers had no basis for comparison with other armies. In the later campaigns, material superiority and experience substantially reduced them, though they remained high compared to what allies and enemies alike regarded as acceptable.

Apart from the first weeks, when some units fled in panic, there was nothing resembling the breakdown of discipline that disrupted the Russian army in 1917, though there were numerous instances in 1941–42 when NKVD troops were stationed behind the front-line soldiers, to shoot any who ran away. Unlike in World War I, no cases were recorded of collective refusal to obey orders. This owed something to the regime's greater ruthlessness, but probably more to indoctrination. Unlike its predecessor, the Red Army, through its political officers, took much trouble to tell the troops why they were at war, and to inculcate hatred of the invader.

Distorted and propagandistic though much of this indoctrination was, it motivated the troops more than the Tsarist dogma that to explain the Tsar's decisions undermined his right to unconditional obedience. Communist values were not particularly emphasized; membership of the Communist Party was not easily granted, and most troops were below the minimum age for membership. However, Communist Party members in the armed forces were expected to set an example to the rest, and many set one good enough for soldiers' applications to join the Party to rise, especially on the eve of major campaigns.

Morale was sustained by several factors, most basic of them patriotic outrage at the fact of invasion and at the atrocities committed by the invader. Propaganda encouraged the soldiers to expect victory to bring radical changes for the better in politics and living standards. The cult of Stalin was all-pervading, but it was only in films that soldiers went into battle shouting "For the Motherland! For Stalin!" Many would, much later, admit putting more trust in God, others that they went into the assault shouting obscenities. One who ended the war in Berlin recollected that:

...luxuries such as leave seldom came our way. Food was monotonous but usually adequate, clothing, especially for winter, much better than the Germans had, but small amenities such as playing cards, dominoes, writing materials or musical instruments were scarce, and usually the first things we looted when we took a German position. Correspondence was censored, and we learned not to criticize our leaders, especially Stalin, because such criticisms attracted heavier punishment than disclosure of military secrets. We knew few of those anyway, because we were only told what we were going to do at the last moment, or sometimes not at all, and the command we mostly heard from our officers was just "follow me." Most of our officers earned our respect for their readiness to lead, but we wished they had been trained to do more than just take us to attack the Germans head on. We respected the Germans as soldiers, and to begin with many of us doubted our own propaganda about German atrocities. But when we began recapturing territory and seeing what they had done there, we came to hate them, and when we reached German soil some of us vented our hatred on German civilians, even on some who claimed to be Communists, in ways I still shudder to think of. As the war ended, Stalin ordered us to change our attitude to the German people, and even to start feeding them. That did cut down the amount of murder and rape, but it didn't stop us looting, or beating up any Germans who didn't accept that they were the losers.

Propaganda, Lend-Lease, and land grabs

Both contestants were totalitarian dictatorships, and did their utmost to control the information their subjects received. The Germans made listening to enemy radio broadcasts a capital offence, the Soviets simply confiscated private radios and set up loudspeakers in public places to broadcast official announcements and heavily censored news. Both enrolled the arts in the war effort, especially their great musical traditions, but very few wartime compositions made it into the permanent repertoire. The outstanding exception, Shostakovich's Seventh Symphony, was partly composed in Leningrad, completed in Kuybyschev after the composer was evacuated, and given its first performance in the besieged city in 1942.

Film and theater were naturally exploited by both sides, but neither produced anything to rival the prewar German *Triumph of the Will* or Soviet *Alexander Nevsky*. Poster art was extensively employed by each side to demonize the other, German posters initially depicting German racial superiority, then shifting more and more to present the campaign in the east as the defense of European civilization against a barbarian Bolshevik–Jewish horde. Soviet posters invoked defense of women and children, or of cities such as Leningrad and Moscow, and the spirits of past heroes, then as the war turned in favor of the Allies depicted Germany, personified by a caricatured Hitler, as being strangled by the flags of the three major Allies, or nipped by three sets of pincers. Like film, the poster art heavily emphasized specifically Russian historical features, rather than Communist values, except for the occasional inclusion of Lenin among great past figures, or the contribution of

other "fraternal" peoples of the multi-ethnic Soviet Union.

Weapons science played an enormous part in the war, but its greatest achievements, the German V-1 cruise missile, V-2 rocket and first jet combat aircraft, and the Anglo-American atomic bomb project found no roles on the Eastern Front. The Soviet T-34 medium tank was superior to the German Marks III and IV, and needed only a modest upgrading of gun and turret to match the new-generation Panther that came into service in 1943. When the Germans introduced the Tiger heavy tank in that year, it outclassed the Soviet KV-1, but the new Soviet JS-1 matched the Tiger in fire power and more than matched it for mobility. Soviet aircraft designers produced fighters of adequate quality and in sufficient numbers to gain permanent air superiority by 1943, and the Il-2 "Shturmovik" was a better ground-attack aircraft than anything Germany had.

Soviet war production was greatly helped by aid from the USA and the British Empire. The Red Army's major weakness in 1941 was in command and control, for lack of radio sets and field telephone equipment. Allied supplies included 35,000 radios, 380,000 field telephone sets, 956,000 miles (1,538,491 km) of cable, 14,200 aircraft, and over 438,000 vehicles. This aid, and large numbers of machine tools, enabled Soviet industry to survive the loss of most of its European industrial base, relocate much of it to the Urals and Siberia, and out-produce Germany in tanks and combat aircraft. The value of the Allied aid was universally denigrated in Soviet-period histories, and only in the 1990s was it disclosed that both Stalin and Zhukov had privately conceded that the Soviet

Union could not have continued the war without it.

The Alliance was a shotgun wedding, and once its sole purpose, defeat of the Axis powers, was achieved it quickly fell apart. That the Soviet Union bore the brunt of the war with Germany, and paid by far the heaviest price, is undeniable. The Soviet armed forces total of 8.7 million dead or missing, made public only in the 1990s, was about 11 times US and British Empire losses combined, and almost 20 million Soviet civilians also perished. A Soviet epigram had it that to win the war the British gave time, the Americans money, the Russians blood. The constant Soviet agitation for a Second Front derived from mistrust of capitalist allies, who were seen as happy to have the

Marshals Zhukov and Rokossovsky and subordinates with Field Marshal Montgomery after conferring of British honors. (AKG Berlin)

10 months before the Allies landed in France, and Field Marshal Montgomery later said that in the war's last weeks he was more concerned about the advancing Russians than about the retreating Germans. His fears proved unfounded; the rapid British advance across the base of the Jutland peninsula prevented Soviet occupation of Denmark except for the Baltic island of Bornholm.

Other major bones of contention were Poland and the Baltic States. In the Polish case, Stalin sought Allied acceptance of the Soviet–Polish border established in 1939 under the Molotov–Ribbentrop agreement. He could, and did, cite in support the fact that the frontier very closely matched the "Curzon Line" delineated in 1919 by an international committee chaired by the British Foreign Secretary. As for the Baltic States, Estonia, Latvia, and Lithuania, he sought recognition of their annexation in 1940.

Further problems arose in Polish–Soviet relations when in April 1943 the Germans announced discovery of the mass graves of several thousand Polish officers at Katyn, near Smolensk, apparently shot not later than April 1940: that is, while in Soviet hands. The Soviets claimed that the Germans had shot them after occupying the area in 1941, and when the Polish government in exile in London disagreed, Stalin broke off relations with it. Almost 50 years later, Moscow admitted that 21,857 Polish officer prisoners had indeed been murdered in early 1940 on Stalin's orders.

The West could do little. The Soviet Union's pivotal role in the war against Germany inhibited public airing of differences, and the countries in question were all reconquered by the Red Army, putting the Soviet position beyond challenge. Poland was compensated with German territory; the Baltic States regained their independence only when the Soviet Union collapsed.

Soviet Union bled white, but also from ignorance of what a major seaborne invasion entailed.

A standard accusation of some Soviet and post-Soviet Russian historians is that the Allies mounted the Second Front only from fear that otherwise the Red Army could occupy (and Communize) western Europe. Germany's retreat in the east indeed began

"We were as mobilized as the soldiers"

The Sicherheitsdienst (Security Service) monitored German civilian attitudes through about 25,000 informants, collating the findings in twice-weekly reports. These showed that underneath public euphoria was a deep vein of skepticism (for example, "In the First World War too we were winning at the start"), and disdain for Nazi Party officials, whom the public dubbed *Goldfasanen* (Golden Pheasants). Germany did not switch to a full war economy until after Stalingrad. Propaganda Minister Goebbels, addressing a rally in Berlin two weeks after the surrender there, received a roar of "Yes!" to his rhetorical question "Do you want total war?" but not all Germans were as enthusiastic; a verse from the Ruhr pleaded to RAF bomber crews: "Dear Tommy, please fly further. We're all miners here. Fly on to Berlin – they're the ones who all shouted 'Yes.'" German civilian life was more seriously affected by bombing than by the Eastern Front, until the Red Army reached East Prussia late in 1944. Then news of the retribution being exacted for German atrocities prompted a flood of refugees.

German obedience to authority, nurtured by long exposure to despotic but generally benign rulers, served the Nazis well – surviving even the imposition of the death penalty for listening to enemy broadcasts – and so, paradoxically, did civilian skepticism. Because their expectations were not high, they were not shattered by misfortune. Morale until very late withstood both bombing and the setbacks that began in November 1942; and while in the last days many almost totally untrained Volkssturm and Hitler Youth detachments ran away or surrendered, others fought ferociously to the end.

The Russian civilian was as mobilized as the soldier. The working day was increased to 12 hours, days off were reduced from one a week to one a month, and rations gave preference to production workers over the old, very young, or disabled. To control information, radio sets were confiscated, and replaced by loudspeakers set up in public places to retail official pronouncements. Associating with even Allied foreigners, absenteeism, late arrival at work, or failure to fulfil quotas could result in a long sentence to forced labor in the "Gulag," prison, or a corrective labor camp. In 1943 a new punishment, "hard labor," was introduced for the worst offenders; it usually meant death by overwork and malnutrition.

Peasants did not receive ration cards; they had to subsist on what they grew in their private plots, and what their collective farm could provide after fulfilling its delivery quotas. Conscription of males and commandeering of horses left production by mostly unmechanized agriculture to women and males who were too old, too young, or unfit for military service. Plows pulled by teams of women were a not uncommon sight, and so, in the cities, was a tolerated "free market," where peasants lucky enough to have any surplus food could sell it for high prices. Urban dwellers with dachas (suburban plots) grew additional food there, but often found it stolen. In 1944 a system for guarding plots, and the death penalty for stealing food, were introduced. A Muscovite woman, a schoolgirl at the time, recalled that:

we had been told day and night that our army was invincible, and were shocked at how fast the Germans advanced in the first months. In October the older classes in my school were among those sent to dig trenches on the outskirts of the city. We heard that many people ran away from Moscow in mid-month, but didn't see any sign of it ourselves. There were many air raids; no bombs fell near where we lived, but the noise of the anti-aircraft guns sometimes made it hard to sleep; anyway the air raids stopped after a few months.

With father away in the army, and mother working 12 hours in a bakery, we children had mostly to look after ourselves, though mother's job meant we didn't have to join the queues for bread; neighbors told us they started queuing before dawn. We always had enough to eat, but had to spend a lot of time in queues at the food shops. Getting clothes and shoes as we grew bigger was difficult; we were told it was because the factories were too busy making uniforms and boots for the soldiers. We lived in a big apartment with one family to every room, and shared the kitchen and bathroom. A lot of the housing in Moscow was like that; it was long after the war that we got a flat to ourselves. Some of the other children in the apartment lost their fathers or brothers at the front, but we were lucky. Father survived the war, and my brother wasn't old enough to be called up, though in the last two years he had to work in a plant that made radio parts.

By then we were throwing the Germans out, and when we heard gunfire we knew it wasn't an air raid, it was a victory salute to celebrate the capture of some town. We didn't go to the victory parade because it rained all day, but we saw it on a newsreel, and everybody cheered when we saw the German army banners thrown in a heap at Stalin's feet. We idolized him then.

Germany surrenders, Stalin joins the war on Japan

Berlin surrendered on May 2, 1945; Hitler had committed suicide two days earlier, appointing Grand Admiral Dönitz as his successor. Dönitz sent Colonel-General Jodl and Admiral Friedeburg to Reims to negotiate surrender. It was to all the Allies, but Stalin considered that a surrender to Eisenhower denigrated the Soviet role in the war, and insisted on having a formal surrender ceremony in Berlin. This took place on the evening of May 8 at a ceremony in Berlin presided over by Marshal Zhukov, who signed on the Soviet Union's behalf. All German forces had surrendered by May 16. Now Japan's turn had come.

On June 3 the State Defense Committee decided to redeploy troops to the Far East, and to build up ammunition, fuel, food, and fodder stocks for the campaign against Japan, which Stalin had agreed the Soviet Union would enter within three months of victory in Europe. The Allied leaders met at Potsdam on July 17, and on July 26 the US, British, and Chinese governments issued the Potsdam Declaration, demanding that Japan surrender unconditionally. Stalin was annoyed at not being consulted, but subscribed to it later. The noncommittal Japanese reply was interpreted as a rejection, so the Soviet Union went to war with Japan on August 9.

From alliance to Cold War

In 1938, when the British and French Prime Ministers met the German and Italian dictators at Munich to decide Czechoslovakia's fate, the Soviet Union was not invited. In 1945 Stalin hosted the Potsdam Conference of Allied leaders in Berlin, which his troops had captured 12 weeks previously. They had played the decisive role in defeating Germany, and had brought Soviet power into central Europe.

This was accomplished by a regime so oppressive that many of its subjects welcomed the invaders, and its soldiers initially surrendered in unprecedented numbers. Over 600,000 of them served the German army as auxiliaries, over 50,000 joined the turncoat General Vlasov's "Russian Liberation Army." Many Ukrainians, Cossacks, Balts, Caucasians, and central Asians joined the Waffen SS, or the various "Legions" raised by the Germans, or served as guards and executioners in extermination camps.

That this regime survived disasters far exceeding those that brought down Tsarism in 1917 owed much to its ruthlessness, but more to other factors. These included the industrialization Stalin initiated in 1931, the talents of the managers and designers it produced, and, after Stalin's Civil War cronies, Voroshilov, Budenny, and Kulik, proved incompetent, the professionalism of younger generals, mostly in their forties. Other factors included a General Staff that became a very efficient tool for Stalin's direction of the war. Intelligence and counterintelligence significantly out-performed their German counterparts. Like the British, the Soviets succeeded in killing or "turning" all German spies on their territory; so information reaching the Abwehr or Foreign Armies East was systematically "doctored," whereas Soviet agents in Germany provided a steady flow of high-quality information. The Soviets may also have solved the German "Enigma" cipher

A Ukrainian woman welcoming German troops, 1941. (AKG Berlin)

German Army Cossacks belonging to the largest among several "Foreign Legions" that the Germans raised from among Soviet prisoners of war. (AKG Berlin)

machine early in 1943, but even if they did not, the British passed on information from deciphered messages, and so did some of the "famous five" spies, Philby, Blunt, Cairncross, McLean, and Burgess.

Two external factors that also affected the war in the east were Allied bombing and Allied, especially American, aid. During the Cold War, Soviet writers customarily disparaged the Allied contribution and questioned Allied motivation, citing the delays in mounting the "Second Front," and quoting *ad nauseam* Senator, later President, Truman's statement of July 1941 that when the Germans were winning, the USA should help the Russians, and when the Russians were winning, it should help the Germans. Allied bombing, though it began delivering the expected results only in the final year, diverted two-thirds of German fighter aircraft and anti-aircraft guns from supporting the army to defending Germany, and a similar proportion of aircraft production from bombers and ground-attack aircraft to fighters. From mid-1944 attacks on the hydrogenation plants that produced oil from coal, and on transport arteries, severely reduced German mobility, while 438,000 American-supplied vehicles greatly enhanced the Red Army's. Allied supplies of vehicles, machine tools, aircraft, railway equipment, radios, cable, raw materials, textiles, and food enabled Soviet industry to focus on out-producing Germany in tanks, guns, and aircraft.

The most powerful single factor in the victory was Russian patriotism. Stalin quickly sensed its importance, and his speeches became replete with invocations of past Russian victories and victors. Persecution of religion ceased, Tsarist officer ranks and insignia, and the title of "Guards" were revived, and names of past heroes were used for new medals and as codenames for major offensives. Even where initially welcomed, the Germans outwore their welcome by their brutality, and in any case preference for native over foreign oppressors is implicit in the Russian proverb "Pust khuzhe da nashe" ("Let it be worse, provided it's ours").

Soviet soldiers undoubtedly fought in expectation of a better postwar world, but Stalin continued to make war on his people long after Germany's defeat. Ex-prisoners of war, troops escaped from behind enemy lines, and civilians from formerly occupied areas underwent lengthy interrogations, often followed by imprisonment, and so did many partisans, simply because they had lived where the Soviet writ temporarily did not run. Several small nations were deported *en masse* to Siberia or central Asia, the Volga Germans in 1941, the Karachais, Crimean Tartars, Chechens, Ingush, Kalmyks, and Meskhetians after reconquest of the Caucasus and Crimea in 1943–44, because some of them collaborated with the invaders. The total deported in 1943–44 was at least 1.5 million. Stalin's refusal to support the Warsaw Rising, and his recognition as government of Poland of a Communist "national committee" that enjoyed little Polish support was in a sense the first act of the Cold War.

The victories his generals gained made them dispensable. Fearing their popularity, and to emphasize his own role as a military leader, Stalin revived for himself the rank of Generalissimus, extinct since 1800, just before joining the war against Japan, and in his victory speech on September 2, 1945, he presented himself as avenging Russia's defeat by Japan in the war of 1904–05. Until after his death, the retreat to the Volga was depicted as deliberate, luring the enemy on the better to destroy him, like Kutuzov in 1812.

The most successful marshals were posted far from Moscow and each other: Zhukov went to a provincial command, Rokossovsky and Konev to command Soviet forces in Poland and Hungary, and Malinovsky was kept in the Far East until 1951. Stalin did not arrest Zhukov, but had numerous lesser lights arrested and tortured to testify to a nonexistent "Bonapartist" conspiracy headed by him. Novikov, the air force Commander-in-Chief, was imprisoned on additional trumped-up charges of sabotaging aircraft production; naval Commander-in-

Chief Kuznetsov was dismissed and demoted; and three other admirals were imprisoned on charges that included giving maps of Soviet harbors to the British – the maps were Russian copies of British Admiralty charts.

The victors imposed their social order wherever their armies went, but the democracy imposed by the Anglo-Americans proved more acceptable and, ultimately, more durable than the Communism of eastern Europe or of the Soviet Union itself. But that outcome was preceded by four decades of Cold War between the alliance systems created by the two countries elevated to superpower status by World War II.

Soviet military capability tended to be as overestimated in that period as it had been underestimated prewar, and anti-Soviet canards were propagated, such as that the western allies demobilized but the Soviet Union did not, and that its objective was world domination. Ample evidence was available at the time that masses of Soviet troops were heading home in summer 1945 for discharge, in everything from horse-drawn carts to freight trains. With 70,000 destroyed villages and 1,200 towns to rebuild, and collective farms run for the past three years by women, children, the old, and the disabled, the soldiers were needed in civilian life. The Soviet armed forces, numbering 11,365,000 at the war's end, were back by 1948 to their 1939 level of just under 3 million. Only after Stalin's death would his successor, Khrushchev, proclaim war between capitalism and Communism no longer inevitable, but Stalin did not believe it imminent, and probably did not believe it inevitable either. One of his last pronouncements was that a third world war would, like the first two, more likely be between the capitalist countries than between capitalism and Communism.

As for world domination, Communism claimed to be historically destined for universal adoption, but had no timetable for it; nor did Stalin commit the Soviet Union to fight a war for it. His expansionism was opportunist, aimed at restoring as far as possible the frontiers of the former Empire, establishing subservient states in the east European corridor through which all Russia's invaders except the Mongols had come, and weakening western positions elsewhere if that could be done at low risk.

In Germany he tested Anglo-American resolve in 1948 by blocking access to Berlin, cautiously not proclaiming a ban, but declaring all rail, road, and water access routes simultaneously closed for repairs. The western powers surprised him by mounting an airlift to supply their sectors; it experienced only some "buzzing" by Soviet aircraft, and the Berlin Air Safety Center continued to operate. Had the Soviet controllers been withdrawn, the airlift could have operated only in daylight, and might have failed, prompting the more confrontational western riposte that some American generals advocated. When Stalin realized it could continue indefinitely, and was bringing the West propaganda advantage, he declared all surface routes repaired and reopened.

Alarm bells rang in the West when Communist victory in China in October 1949 was followed in June 1950 by Communist North Korea's invasion of the south. The belief that both were implementing a plan devised in Moscow was, however, erroneous. Stalin did not believe a true Communist movement could be built, as was the Chinese one, on peasants rather than on industrial workers, and in 1946 he had advised the Chinese Communists against initiating a civil war.

The North Korean leader, Kim Il-sung, persuaded Stalin and Mao in 1950 that the South Korean masses would rise in his support if his Soviet-equipped army invaded, so both assumed South Korea would fall before the West reacted. When that proved wrong, Stalin confined Soviet participation to some Mig-15 jet fighters and pilots, happily saw China join the war, but sent it a bill for everything he supplied. He took no action even after US aircraft bombed a Soviet airfield near the border, and refrained from further provocative acts up to his death in March 1953.

Glossary

Axis The alliance of Germany and Italy, and eastern nations such as Japan, during World War II.

Baltic Of or relating to the Baltic Sea or surrounding areas.

Berlin The capitol of Germany.

Bolshevik A member of the Russian Communist party.

Communism A political system in which all property is owned by the community, and each member of the community works and is paid by their ability and means.

counteroffensive A major attack made in response to an attack.

Czechoslovakia A former country in central Europe, which is now divided between the Czech Republic and Slovakia.

Danzig German name of Gdańsk, a city in northern Poland.

Estonia A country on the southern coast of the Gulf of Finland.

field marshal The highest-ranking officer in many countries' armies.

Georgia A country in southeastern Europe on the shore of the Black Sea.

Hermann Wilhelm Goering German Nazi leader and politician who was sentenced to death at the Nuremberg war trials.

Adolf Hitler German totalitarian leader who established the Nazi party.

Infantry Soldiers marching on foot.

Leningrad The former name for St. Petersburg, a city in northwestern Russia.

Muscovite A native of the city of Moscow.

Nazi A member or follower of the Nazi party.

Potsdam Conference A meeting that took place during the summer of 1945 between US, Soviet, and British leaders that laid the groundwork for the Allied occupation of Germany after World War II.

propaganda Information that is designed to mislead or misinform.

Prussia A former kingdom of Germany, it was once a major European power.

reconnaissance Military observation of a region to analyze its strategic features.

Red Square A large square in Moscow next to the Kremlin.

ruse de guerre A French term meaning "ruse of war," or "trick of war," an action designed to deceive the opponent.

sabotage To deliberately destroy something for military gain.

Socialist A political system that calls for the means of production to be regulated by the community.

Soviet Union A group of Communist republics that was created in the aftermath of the 1917 Russian Revolution and was dissolved in 1991 after economic failure.

Ukraine A country in Eastern Europe north of the Black Sea.

For More Information

National World War II Memorial
National Park Service
900 Ohio Drive SW
Washington, DC 20024
(202) 426-6841
Web site: http://www.wwiimemorial.com/
One of the most treasured landmarks in
Washington, D.C., the National World
War II Memorial commemorates the 16
million who served in the armed forces
of the US, and the more than 400,000
who died.

U.S. Department of Defense
1400 Defense Pentagon
Washington, D.C. 20301-1400
(703) 428-0711
Web site: http://www.defenselink.mil/
The Department of Defense is the federal
organization responsible for overseeing
the United States military and the safety
of the country.

The Wright Museum
77 Center Street
Wolfeboro, NH 03894-4368
(603) 569-1212
Web site: http://www.wrightmuseum.org
Located in Wolfeboro, NH, the Wright
Museum's mission is to "preserve and
share the stories of America's Greatest
Generation," which served in World
War II.

National Military History Center
P.O. Box 1
Auburn, IN 46706
(260) 927-9144
Web site:
   http://www.militaryhistorycenter.org/
The National Military History Center
   commemorates those who served in
   World War II.

Museum of World War II
46 Eliot Street
Natick, MA 01760
(508) 651-7695
Web site:
   http://www.museumofworldwarii.com/
With 10,000 square feet of display area, it is
   described by London's Imperial War
   Museum as "a fully staffed private collection
   containing the most comprehensive display
   of original World War II artifacts on exhibit
   anywhere in the world."

The National World War II Museum
945 Magazine Street
New Orleans, LA 70130
(504) 527-6012
Web site: http://www.ddaymuseum.org/
Founded by renowned historian, author and
   educator, Stephen Ambrose, the National
   World War II Museum Foundation
   addresses all of the amphibious invasions
   of World War II.

Web Sites
Due to the changing nature of Internet links,
Rosen Publishing has developed an online
list of Web sites related to the subject of this
book. This site is updated regularly. Please
use this link to access the list:

http://www.rosenlinks.com/wweh/east

For Further Reading

Adams, Simon. *The Eastern Front* (Documenting World War II). New York, NY: Rosen Publishing Group, Inc., 2008.

Adams, Simon. *World War II* (DK Eyewitness Books). New York, NY: Dorling Kindersley, 2007.

Battistelli, Pier Paolo. *Panzer Divisions 1944–45*. Oxford, England: Osprey Publishing, 2009.

Conway, John Richard. *Primary Source Accounts of World War II* (America's Wars Through Primary Sources). Berkeley Heights, NJ: Enslow Publishers, Inc., 2006

Doeden, Matt. *Weapons of World War II* (Blazers). Mankato, MN: Capstone Press, 2008.

Grant, Reg. *World War II* (DK Readers). New York, NY: Dorling Kindersley, 2008.

Jurado, Carlos Caballero. *Blue Division Soldier 1941–45: Spanish Volunteer on the Eastern Front*. Oxford, England: Osprey Publishing, 2009.

Keegan, John. *The Second World War*. New York, NY: Penguin, 2005.

Layson, Annelex Hofstra. *Lost Childhood: My Life in a Japanese Prison Camp During World War II*. Washington, DC: National Geographic Books, 2008.

Matthews, Rupert. *World Wars* (Timelines). Essex, England: Miles Kelly Publishing, 2008.

Murray, Doug. *D-Day* (Graphic Battles of World War II). New York, NY: Rosen Publishing Group, Inc., 2007.

O'Shei, Tim. *World War II Spies* (Edge Books). Mankato, MN: Capstone Press, 2008.

Panchyk, Richard, and Senator John McCain. *World War II for Kids: A History with 21 Activities*. Chicago, IL: Chicago Review Press, 2002.

Wagner, Margaret E. *The Library of Congress World War II Companion*. New York, NY: Simon & Schuster, 2007.

Bibliography

History of the Second World War, London, Purnell,1966–69, vols 3–8.

Barnett, C. (ed.), *Hitler's Generals*, London, Weidenfeld & Nicolson.

Overy, R., *Russia's War*, London, Allen Lane, 1998.

Shukman, H. (ed.), *Stalin's Generals*, London, Weidenfeld & Nicolson, 1993.

Zhukov, G. K., *The Memoirs of Marshal Zhukov*, London, Jonathan Cape, 1971.

Index

Allies 9, 11, 14, 48, 51, 54-55, 59, 61, 62, 66, 71-72, 78,
  81-83, 86, 89, 90
  Potsdam Conference 12, 87
  Tehran Conference 10
Ardennes offensive 62
armistices 11, 14, 59, 62, 70-71
atrocities 62
Austria 12, 13, 65, 66

"Bagration" offensives 10, 54-59, 61
Baltic operation 10, 61
Barvenkovo offensive 35
Belorussia 5, 7, 9, 23, 54, 55
Berlin 11, 12, 14, 63, 65, 86, 90
  battle of 12, 66-67
Bock, Field Marshal von 19, 23, 35, 36-37, 38
Bolshevik Revolution 5
  anniversary celebrations 30
Bor-Komorowski, General 56-57
Brauchitsch, Field Marshal 5, 25, 35
Britain 5, 12, 13, 14, 87
  see also Allies
Bryansk 25, 26
Budenny, Marshal 29
Bulgaria 10, 59
Busch, Field Marshal 54, 55

Carpathians
  East 10, 54, 61
  West 11
casualties 8, 9, 10, 23, 26, 27, 29, 32-33, 35, 36, 38, 43,
  44-46, 47, 48, 49, 51-52, 54, 55, 57, 63, 64, 66, 77
Caucasus 35, 36
  battle for 8
  German withdrawal from 9, 46
China 12, 90
Chir River 43
Churchill, Winston 11, 14, 49, 57, 62, 66, 72
Chuykov, V. I., Lieutenant-General 38-40, 67, 71
civilians 84-85
  see also partisan warfare
Cold War 87-90
collaboration 10, 12, 89
communications 22
  see also propaganda
Communism 30, 80, 90
Crimea 7, 9, 12, 51, 54
"Curzon Line" 13-14
Czechoslovakia 10, 12, 13, 66, 71

desertion 78-79
Dietrich, Otto 29-30
Dnepr River 19, 25
  battle for 9, 10, 49-51, 52
Don River 8, 35, 36-37, 38, 40, 42, 46
Donets River 9, 33-34, 46
Dönitz, Admiral 71, 86

Eisenhower, Dwight D. 12, 66
Estonia 5, 7, 11, 14, 54, 61

Finland 5, 7, 10, 14, 19, 52, 59
France 13, 14, 51, 59
Friedeburg, Admiral von 71, 86
Friessner, General 56, 61
Frisches Haff 11, 12

Gehlen, Colonel 42
Goering, Hermann 42, 43

Guderian, Inspector-General 14, 23, 25, 26, 27, 35,
  46, 62

Halder, Colonel-General 25, 38, 42
Heinrici, Colonel-General 64, 66
Hitler, Adolf 6, 7, 9, 13, 14, 18, 23, 33, 35, 38, 42, 43,
  44, 46, 47, 48-49, 50, 51, 52, 55, 56, 59, 61, 62, 64,
  66, 70, 78, 81
  Directives 22, 23, 38
Hitler Youth 66, 84
Hoepner, Colonel-General 23, 27, 35
Hoth, Herman, Colonel-General 23, 27, 37, 43, 44, 50
Hungary 7, 8, 10, 11, 61-62, 64-65

Ilchenko, Lieutenant 44
Italy 7, 8, 48, 49

Japan 6, 9, 11, 12, 30, 71-72, 74-75, 86
Jodl, Colonel-General 71, 86

Kalach 8, 42, 43
Kalinin 9, 30
Kharkov 7, 49
  battle of 8
  retaking of 9, 35, 46
Kiev 7, 9, 18, 25, 26, 35, 50
Kirponos, M. P., Colonel-General 17, 24
Kleist, Ewald, Field Marshal von 25, 26, 36, 37
Kluge, Field Marshal 46, 48, 51
Konev, I. S., Marshal 54, 58, 63, 66, 67, 69, 89
Korsun–Shevchenkovsky, battle of 10
Krebs, Hans, Colonel-General 70-71
Kurile Islands 12, 72, 75
Kurland 11, 12, 61
Kursk 9, 46, 49, 78
Kuznetsov, F. I., Colonel-General 23, 70, 90

Ladoga, Lake 7, 8
Latvia 5, 7, 14
Leeb, Wilhelm Ritter, Field Marshal von 23
Leningrad 18, 21, 23, 35
  siege of 7, 8, 10, 26, 36, 54
Lindemann, Colonel-General 55-56
Lithuania 5, 7, 10, 14, 61
Luftwaffe 20, 21, 43, 50, 66

Malinovsky, R. Y., General 54, 72, 89
Manchukuo (Manchuria) 12, 72-77
Manstein, Colonel-General 5, 9, 37, 43, 44, 46, 48-49,
  51, 58
Meretskov, K. A., Marshal 59, 72
military strength
  Germany 19-20, 21, 23, 24-25, 37, 41, 42, 49-50, 52,
    55, 61, 63
  Soviet Union 20-21, 24, 30, 31, 36, 41, 46-47, 48, 49,
    52, 54, 61, 62-63, 64, 90
mines 40, 46
Minsk 7, 10, 23, 56
Mius River 33, 35
Model, Field Marshal 5, 46, 47, 55
Molotov, Soviet Foreign Minister 13, 14
Montgomery, Field Marshal 66, 83
Moscow 7, 18, 23, 25, 26, 35, 38, 71, 78
  battle of 8
  siege of 7, 29-33
Mozhaisk 29, 30

Nazism 62, 78
Neisse River 11, 67

Neutrality Pact (1941) 12
Norway 11, 14

Oder River 11, 12
  see also Vistula–Oder offensive
Odessa 21
  siege of 7
Operation Barbarossa 22, 23
Operation Citadel 9, 46-49
Operation Fridericus 36
Operation Herman 51
Operation Koltso ("Ring") 44
Operation Kutuzov 9, 48
Operation Rumyantsev 49
Operation Suvorov-1 49
Operation Typhoon 7, 27, 29
Order 227 8, 40
Orel salient 49

partisan warfare 51-52, 54
Paulus, Colonel-General 9, 37, 43, 44
Pavlov, D. G. Army General 23
Ploesti 23, 54, 58-59, 61
Poland 5, 6, 11, 14, 14, 23, 56-57, 63-64, 83, 89
Pomerania 11, 63
Potsdam Declaration 12, 86
prisoners of war 7, 10, 23, 25, 26, 56, 62, 65, 78
Prokhorovka, battle of 9, 46, 48, 78
propaganda 30, 81
Prussia, East 11, 14, 56, 61
purges, military 18, 35
Purkayev, Army General M. A. 72

Red Army 5, 19, 20-21, 49, 54, 78-80
Reichenau, Field Marshal von 35
Reims 12, 71
Reinhard, General 55, 63
Ribbentrop, German Foreign Minister 13
Richthofen, Baron Wolfram von 43
Rokossovsky, K. K., Marshal 22, 40, 47, 44, 46, 51, 55, 56, 63, 66, 67, 89
Romanenko, Lieutenant-General 40
Romania 7, 8, 10, 14, 19, 23, 54, 58-59
Roosevelt, Franklin D. 49, 57, 72
Rostov-on-Don 7, 35, 38
Rundstedt, Gerd, Field Marshal von 19, 23, 25, 35
Rybalko, General P. 69-70

Schoerner, General of Mountain Troops 51, 61, 63
Sevastopol 8, 21, 10
  siege of 7

Shaposhnikov, Chief of General Staff 31-32
Shumilov, General 44
Sigulda Line 61
Slovakia 10, 59
Smolensk 9
  battle of 7
spies 14, 30, 87-89
Stalin, Joseph 6, 7, 9, 11, 12, 13, 14-17, 18, 24, 25-26, 29, 30, 32, 35, 36, 37-38, 40, 41, 42, 46, 47, 54, 57, 59, 62, 63, 66, 67, 70, 71, 72-74, 75, 78-79, 80, 81, 83, 85, 86, 87, 89, 90
Stalingrad 8, 9, 35, 38-44, 78
supplies 7, 8, 30, 31, 33, 35, 38, 40, 41, 42, 43, 44, 46, 49, 52, 57, 61, 65, 81-82, 89

Timoshenko, Marshal 14, 17, 20, 22, 35-37
Tolbukhin, F. I., Marshal 66

Ukraine 5, 18, 23, 24, 26
Uman "pocket" 7, 25
United States of America *see* Allies

Vasilevsky, A. M., Marshal 12, 40, 41, 42, 50, 54, 72, 74
Vatutin, N. F., Lieutenant-General 40, 46, 47, 51
Versailles Treaty 5, 13
Vilnius 7, 10, 56
Vistula–Oder offensive 11, 62-64
Vitebsk 55
Vlasov, General 71
Volga River 8, 35, 38, 40
Volkssturm 66, 84
Voronezh 8, 35, 38
Voroshilov, Minister Kliment 6, 17-18, 20
Vyazma "pocket" 7, 27

Warsaw 10, 11, 56, 63
weather conditions 29, 30, 33, 35, 43, 44, 46, 47, 50
Weichs, Field Marshal 38, 43
Weidling, General 71

Yamada, General 12
Yeremenko, A. I., General 26, 39, 40, 43-44, 54
Yugoslavia 10, 11, 22, 59, 61, 62

Zeitzler, Kurt, General 42
Zhukov, G. K., General 7, 8, 9, 14, 22, 25, 26, 27, 29, 30, 31-32, 40, 41, 42, 46, 47, 49, 54, 58, 63, 66, 67, 69, 71, 72, 81-82, 86, 89

About the Authors

Professor Robert O'Neill, AO D.PHIL. (Oxon), Hon D. Litt.(ANU), FASSA, Fr Hist S, is the Series Editor of Essential Histories. His wealth of knowledge and expertise shapes the series content and provides up-to-the-minute research and theory. Born in 1936 an Australian citizen, he served in the Australian army (1955-68) and has held a number of eminent positions in history circles, including the Chichele Professorship of the History of War at All Souls College, University of Oxford, 1987-2001, and the Chairmanship of the Board of the Imperial War Museum and the Council of the International Institute for Strategic Studies, London. He is the author of many books including works on the German Army and the Nazi party, and the Korean and Vietnam wars. Now based in Australia on his retirement from Oxford he is the Chairman of the Council of the Australian Strategic Policy Institute.

After leaving Oxford in 1953 Geoffrey Jukes spent 14 years in the UK Ministry of Defense and Foreign and Colonial Office, specializing in Russian/Soviet military history, strategy, and arms control. From 1967 to 1993 he was also on the staff of the Australian National University. He has written five books and numerous articles on the Eastern Front in the two world wars.